GREG GEORGE

THE SCIENCE OF INTERPERSONAL RELATIONS

Unlocking the Secrets to Building Strong and
Meaningful Connections
(2024 Guide for Beginners)

Copyright © 2024 by Greg George

All rights reserved. No part of this publication may be reproduced, stored or transmitted in any form or by any means, electronic, mechanical, photocopying, recording, scanning, or otherwise without written permission from the publisher. It is illegal to copy this book, post it to a website, or distribute it by any other means without permission.

First edition

This book was professionally typeset on Reedsy.
Find out more at reedsy.com

Contents

1. Introduction: The Importance of Enhancing Your Interpersonal... — 1
2. Part I: Laying the Groundwork For Healthy Relationships — 7
3. Chapter 1: The Role of Effective Communication in Selecting... — 8
4. Chapter 2: Identifying & Handling Codependency — 16
5. Chapter 3: Setting & Defending Boundaries In A Relationship — 22
6. Chapter 4: Defining A Relationship — 29
7. Chapter 5: Your Partner's Most Important Need, & How To Meet... — 35
8. Chapter 6: How To Make Assertive Communication Work In Your... — 41
9. Chapter 7: How to Identify & Handle Verbal Abuse — 48
10. Chapter 8: Dealing with Negative People — 55
11. Chapter 9: Identifying & Handling Love Addiction — 63
12. Part II: Enhancing the Communication Abilities Necessary for... — 70
13. Chapter 10: Understanding Different Communication Styles — 71
14. Chapter 11: How to Validate Another Person (And Yourself!) — 80
15. Chapter 12: How to Say "No" To Anyone — 88
16. Chapter 13: How to Stop Having The Same Old Arguments — 95
17. Chapter 14: Topics Couples Fight About Most Often — 101
18. Chapter 15: How to Use Communication To Rebuild Trust &... — 108
19. Chapter 16: Communication Tools That Will Rekindle the Flame... — 113
20. Chapter 17: Effective Communication for Parents & Caregivers — 116
21. Chapter 18: Communication Strategies for Friendships — 120

22 Conclusion

1

Introduction: The Importance of Enhancing Your Interpersonal Abilities

By the time we reach the end of high school, most of us have ventured into dating, experiencing love at least once along the way. It's evident that romantic relationships hold significant importance. It's logical, considering that our species' enduring interest in love and physical closeness has contributed to our survival. That exhilarating feeling when encountering someone who quickens your heartbeat is incomparable. Love triggers the release of dopamine in the brain, igniting pleasure centers and emphasizing the profound role romantic relationships play in our lives.

However, despite love's innate appeal, why aren't romantic relationships straightforward? They often become complex rapidly, posing one of life's greatest challenges: falling and remaining in love. Many of us have witnessed relationships that once flourished dwindle away, and this isn't mere coincidence. While compatibility is crucial, effective communication emerges as the vital element for fostering enduring intimacy. Learning to authentically connect with others and address their needs facilitates the establishment of profound, lasting bonds.

Psychologists and communication specialists have extensively analyzed the underlying difficulties in relationships, identifying a handful of key issues. The crux of my argument is straightforward: If we collectively prioritize enhancing our communication skills, our romantic lives would undoubtedly improve.

Outlined below are the primary causes of most relationship woes:

1. Unrealistic Expectations: Influenced by pervasive media portrayals, many of us develop skewed perceptions of romantic love, expecting smooth sailing. When relationships encounter even minor hurdles, these inflated expectations can lead to disappointment and disillusionment.
2. Dependency on Partners: Some individuals mistakenly believe their partner should fulfill all their emotional needs, neglecting to seek happiness beyond the relationship. This dependency can breed suffocating and unhealthy dynamics.

The solution lies in learning to effectively communicate our desires, requirements, and boundaries within relationships.

There's a prevalent assumption that if a relationship requires effort, it's not worth maintaining. Couples therapy still carries a stigma, with the common belief that troubled relationships should simply end. Unfortunately, this mindset doesn't foster a constructive approach to conflict resolution. Many relationships could likely be salvaged if both partners possessed effective communication skills.

The remedy? We must learn to engage in productive disagreements and find resolutions to our differences.

Another obstacle is the desire to always be right. Prioritizing "winning" arguments over compromise can severely strain a relationship. When individuals focus solely on their own perspectives without empathizing with their partner's viewpoint, distance inevitably grows. Overcoming this challenge is especially daunting for those raised in competitive cultures where winning arguments is prized over understanding.

The solution? We should view relationships as collaborative endeavors, recognize our partner's communication style, and be willing to express vulnerability by acknowledging our own emotional wounds.

We're currently experiencing a period of significant social and cultural change, particularly regarding gender equality and evolving relationship dynamics. While it's positive that individuals of all genders can now explore diverse relationship roles and pursuits, there's a downside: the loss of traditional relationship norms. In the past, there were clear guidelines dictating dating and courtship rituals, with defined roles for men and women. However, as these norms fade, there's a sense of ambiguity regarding how relationships "should" function.

In today's ever-evolving world, the vast array of options can leave us feeling unsure about what we truly desire in a relationship. Dating now involves more analysis and problem-solving, leading to a level of complexity that can be bewildering.

The remedy? Yes, you guessed it—enhanced communication! Openly discussing our relationship preferences and mastering the art of defining our relationships is the way forward.

Those familiar with my previous works know my fervor for communication skills. Years of studying top communicators worldwide and coaching clients in applying these skills have culminated in my bestselling books, "Communication Skills Training" and "The Science of Effective Communication." The positive feedback from readers has been immensely gratifying, motivating me to continue sharing knowledge. Recognizing the demand for guidance in relationships, I embarked on writing this interpersonal communication guide.

In the book's first segment, you'll cultivate a healthy relationship mindset essential for mature love. You'll navigate early dating stages, establish boundaries, and gracefully handle the pivotal "Where is this relationship going?" conversation. Even if you're currently in a relationship, reassessing your communication approach can deepen your connection with your partner.

Reflecting on my own relationship experiences, I cringe at the petty fights and feelings of emptiness that plagued my dating life in my late teens and early twenties. It wasn't until I delved into the psychology of human interaction that my dating struggles began to make sense.

As you delve into this book, you'll realize your capacity to revolutionize your love life. The latter part of the book delves into specific communication strategies to navigate the toughest relationship challenges. You'll uncover why recurring arguments arise, how to sustain long-term relationship sparks, provide the validation your partner craves, assert boundaries without harming your bond, and more. Much of this advice is relevant not only to romantic relationships but also to friendships and family dynamics.

You might initially find the notion of "communication skills" less than romantic. I, too, found the science behind relationships both fascinating and somewhat disheartening, requiring me to shed many illusions about love, dating, and marriage.

But here's the thing—actively honing your relationship skills is a profoundly romantic endeavor because it paves the way for genuine love. Learning to connect with your partner and actively fostering a safe, joyful relationship ranks among the most loving gestures one can make.

Within a short span of immersing myself in literature about common communication pitfalls in dating, my romantic life took a turn for the better. I observed a noticeable improvement in the attention and hints towards a potential long-term future from the girl I was seeing at the time.

An incident underscored that I was heading in the right direction. We decided on a movie followed by coffee, and it turned out to be an obscure arthouse film, which, to be honest, felt utterly pointless and pretentious to me.

When asked about my opinion on the movie afterward, I hesitated before realizing that at 24, this woman wasn't seeking a negative critique of French subtitled films. What she truly craved was an affirming, constructive conversation that could deepen our connection.

Instead of launching into a critical rant, I expressed gratitude for the experience, highlighted aspects I appreciated, and encouraged her to share her perspective. Only then did I offer constructive criticism, ensuring to respect her viewpoint throughout.

Rather than dissecting the film technically, I shared how it resonated with me emotionally and triggered memories, prompting her to open up about her own past experiences. This exchange strengthened our bond significantly.

Had I not invested time in understanding empathy and validation in relationships, that conversation could have ended on a sour note, leaving her with the impression of my insensitivity. Instead, we continued dating for another year before parting ways due to life circumstances.

Remarkably, we remain friends to this day. Despite her marriage, she acknowledges me as one of the most considerate, understanding partners she's had. All it took was learning to communicate respectfully, empathize with her, and express my opinions without sparking conflict. If I can do it, so can you!

I can't promise you a flawless partner or an impeccable relationship. Beware of anyone claiming to have found perfection because it simply doesn't exist! However, if you absorb and apply the advice in this book, I assure you that your relationships will see significant improvement.

Even if you're currently single, this book holds invaluable insights for you. Don't wait until you're in a relationship to enhance your relationship skills. By investing in self-improvement now, you'll impress future partners with your empathy, warmth, and captivating personality.

While I can't guarantee that everyone will fall head over heels for you, this book will undeniably increase your chances of finding your ideal match. As a true romantic, I firmly believe that there's someone out there for everyone. But as the saying goes, anything worth having requires effort! It's time to examine how you approach relationships closely. Turn the page and embark on this journey of self-discovery.

2

Part I: Laying the Groundwork For Healthy Relationships

Chapter 1: The Role of Effective Communication in Selecting the Ideal Partner

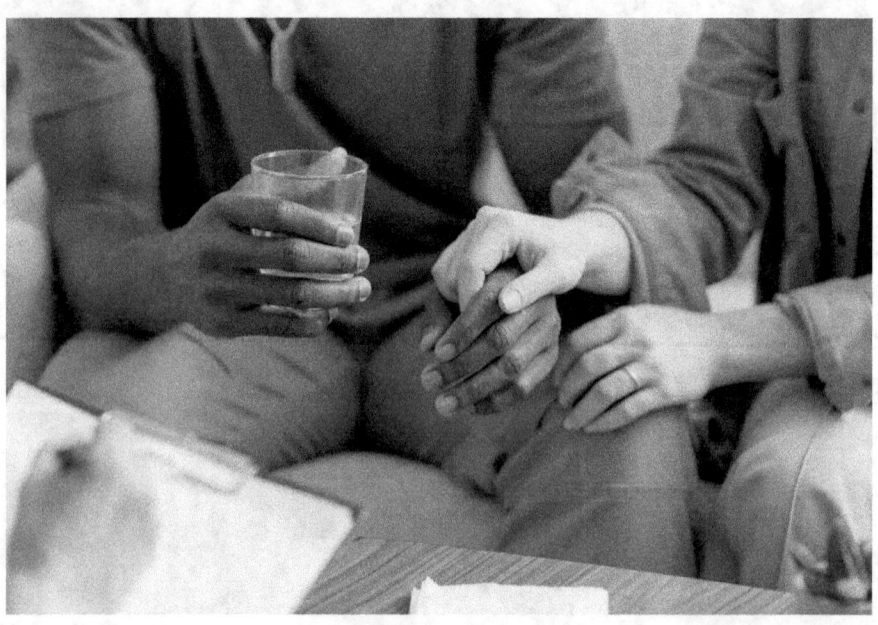

Effective communication skills are not only essential for maintaining a rela-

CHAPTER 1: THE ROLE OF EFFECTIVE COMMUNICATION IN SELECTING...

tionship but also play a pivotal role in selecting the right partner, establishing rapport, and transitioning from the dating phase to a long-term commitment. In this chapter, I will guide you through the strategies necessary to discern incompatible matches, ultimately saving you valuable time.

Early in a relationship, communication skills hold significance in two key aspects. Firstly, you must effectively convey your identity and desires to your potential partner. Secondly, you need to be adept at recognizing signs indicating misalignment or significant emotional and psychological issues in the other person.

Before embarking on the quest for a partner, it's imperative to assess your readiness for dating. Psychological research underscores the necessity of possessing self-awareness, mutual understanding, and emotional regulation skills as prerequisites for healthy relationships. Consider these questions as your preflight checklist:

Question 1:

Are you self-aware of your feelings and clear about your expectations from a partner? Without a clear understanding of your desires, you risk investing time in unsuitable matches. Self-awareness and emotional intelligence are paramount for effective communication in relationships.

Question 2:

Are you open to establishing a relationship based on mutual understanding and compromise? Genuine connections require a willingness to comprehend your partner's perspective and collaborate on solutions during challenging times.

Question 3:

Can you manage your emotions effectively? Emotional regulation is crucial for maintaining relationship harmony. It involves handling discomfort without projecting it onto your partner. Failure to regulate emotions can lead to immature and unhealthy behaviors that strain relationships.

Illustrating this point, I recall my teenage girlfriend, Savannah, who struggled to regulate her emotions. Despite sharing common interests and mutual attraction, her habit of incessantly discussing trivial issues during our time together became draining. This pattern persisted into adulthood for many individuals, highlighting the importance of developing emotional intelligence.

If you find yourself unable to manage your emotions responsibly, it's vital to prioritize personal growth before seeking a relationship. Enhancing your emotional intelligence entails recognizing and coping with emotions effectively, ultimately fostering healthier connections.

Deciphering Signals: Essential Communication Skills for Navigating Early Relationships

Assuming you're prepared for a relationship, it's time to delve into the strategies crucial for the initial stages of dating. Let's outline the objectives for the first few dates:

1. Confirm your date's interest in a relationship.
2. Assess their proficiency in healthy communication.
3. Identify potential red flags.
4. Evaluate fundamental compatibility between you and your date.

I'll address each point individually, guiding you on how to swiftly determine whether pursuing a lasting relationship with your date is worthwhile.

Is your date genuinely seeking a relationship?

CHAPTER 1: THE ROLE OF EFFECTIVE COMMUNICATION IN SELECTING...

The dating scene is diverse, encompassing individuals seeking fleeting connections, those rebounding from past relationships, and those unsure of their relationship goals. While encountering such individuals is inevitable, you can develop skills to identify them early on. Though forming a relationship after just a couple of dates is improbable, you can gauge whether someone seeks a meaningful connection. Here's how to ensure alignment:

Engage in meaningful conversation: Those seeking a genuine connection are eager to learn about their date beyond surface-level topics. Once small talk is surpassed, inquire about their aspirations and dreams. If they reciprocate and display genuine interest in your responses, it's a promising sign. While not a guarantee of commitment, it's a positive start.

Watch for emphasis on physical intimacy: While some successful relationships originate from casual encounters, individuals aiming for long-term partnerships typically don't prioritize immediate physical intimacy. If your date excessively steers conversations toward sexual topics or pressures you regarding preferences, it indicates a focus solely on physical aspects, signaling potential misalignment.

Listen for mentions of ex-partners: References to past relationships should be brief, pertinent, and positive. Multiple references to ex-partners suggest poor relationship judgment, fickleness, or commitment apprehensions. Exercise caution, as this behavior could portend future issues and tarnish your reputation.

By honing these observational skills, you'll be better equipped to discern compatibility and make informed decisions about potential relationships.

Be wary of discussions about future plans that don't align with a committed relationship. When your date mentions upcoming activities, assess whether they've factored in the possibility of a serious relationship. For instance, if they reveal plans to work abroad for six months starting in eight weeks, it's likely they're not seeking a long-term commitment.

If they have definite plans that will consume a significant portion of their time in the near future, there's a straightforward way to discern their intentions: "That sounds exciting! Does it mean you're not looking for anything too serious for a while?"

Pose questions that probe their general outlook on life: Virtually any inquiry can provide insights into your date's personality. For instance, asking about recent books they've read might elicit a pessimistic response from someone with a negative disposition. Even seemingly innocuous queries can unveil aspects of their personality. If they consistently exhibit bitterness or resentment, it's best to part ways, as such negativity isn't conducive to a mature relationship.

Once rapport is established, you can broach the topic of relationship goals. While it's not advisable to start a date with this question, it's appropriate to inquire later if the conversation flows smoothly. If you're hesitant to ask directly, subtly inquire about their aspirations for the next five or ten years. Those seeking a long-term commitment will typically seize the opportunity to share their intentions. Alternatively, you can casually mention marriage or children to gauge their response.

If they express disinterest in a relationship or claim they're not the type to settle down, it's crucial to take them at their word and move on. While there's a slim chance they may change their stance, it's wiser to focus your attention on someone who shares your relationship goals.

Is this individual capable of engaging in healthy communication?

Utilize these strategies to gauge their communication skills and ability to navigate everyday conflicts:

- Inquire about the type of people they associate with or describe their closest friends: Psychological research supports the notion that individuals tend to befriend those similar to themselves, known as "social homophily." Therefore, if your date recounts stories suggesting unpleasant or socially inept friends, it could be a red flag.
- Assess their relationship with their parents: Secure, healthy bonds with parents during childhood often translate into healthy adult relationships. While individuals from troubled family backgrounds can still develop strong communication skills, unresolved issues from their upbringing may pose challenges in relating to others.
- Probe about their family dynamics: A calm, candid discussion about their family situation indicates a level of emotional maturity and resolution of any past grievances. However, extreme dysfunction within their family should prompt caution.
- Inquire about their work environment and relationships with colleagues: Complaints about ongoing workplace conflicts or strained relationships with colleagues may suggest interpersonal deficiencies.
- Present a differing viewpoint and observe their response: While not advocating for needless disagreement, expressing an opposing opinion allows you to gauge their ability to handle differing perspectives. A respectful and empathetic response signals healthy communication skills, while discomfort may indicate a lack of experience in managing disagreements, which could be problematic in the long term.

Are there any warning signs to watch out for?

While some red flags are unmistakable, such as being married or struggling with addiction, others pertain to communication skills. Consider these indicators:

- Inability to apologize: A person who refuses to apologize or distorts the truth may be untrustworthy or even manipulative. Even minor discrepancies in their stories or contradictions should prompt caution.

- Inconsistent communication: If your date alternates between being lively and disengaged without reason, it may indicate insincerity or lack of genuine interest.
- Superficial conversation: If conversations with your date lack depth and substance, it suggests an unwillingness to share personal information, possibly indicating hidden motives.
- Lack of past romantic involvement: If your date claims to have never experienced love despite being well into adulthood, it may raise concerns about their emotional availability or ability to form meaningful connections.
- Every conversation feels like a minefield: Inability to navigate ordinary conversations without tension indicates poor emotional regulation and conflict resolution skills, making them unsuitable for a relationship.

They either demand excessive details too early on or overshare too much information: While encountering someone who readily opens up may seem refreshing compared to aloofness, it often indicates poor boundaries and a lack of understanding of privacy.

Individuals who profess love or discuss long-term commitments early in the dating process likely prefer fantasy over reality, signaling potential trouble ahead. It's best to avoid such situations altogether.

However, these warning signs don't necessarily imply that your date is inherently bad. Sometimes, there may be innocent reasons behind their behavior. For instance, nervousness might lead them to ramble on about superficial topics to make a good impression.

Still, it's essential to weigh your options carefully before giving them the benefit of the doubt. You deserve a partner who is emotionally available and ready for a relationship in the present, not someone who is banking on a future where they've resolved their issues.

Are there any indications that suggest you and your potential partner might

simply be incompatible?

We've all been guilty of overlooking someone's flaws because of physical attraction or a desire to end our single status. It's human nature. However, there are certain points of discord that are insurmountable.

It's crucial to understand that incompatibility doesn't imply that the other person is "bad" or incapable of being a friend; it simply means that you aren't suited to be romantic partners. As a skilled communicator and emotionally mature individual, your responsibility is to recognize these issues early and handle them gracefully.

Let me share a story. My friend Matt met a woman named Sasha while on vacation last year. They spent nearly every moment together, and Matt was thrilled to learn that Sasha lived nearby, hinting at a potential future together. However, on the last night of their trip, Sasha revealed that her daughter would always come first in her life—a fact she had neglected to mention earlier.

Matt, who had made it clear from the start that he didn't want children, realized that this was a fundamental incompatibility. Despite other positive aspects, such as chemistry, Sasha's lack of transparency and their differing views on parenting made a relationship untenable.

Though Matt questioned his decision later, he ultimately understood that compromising on such a crucial matter would only lead to unhappiness in the long run. Recognizing the importance of effective communication and acknowledging irreconcilable differences is essential for a healthy relationship.

Whether it's differences in political beliefs, religious views, attitudes toward parenting, or general life perspectives, some disparities should signal a need to reconsider the relationship. It's challenging to let go of the hope that someone could be the perfect match, but staying grounded in reality is vital for relationship success. Stay observant and attentive to these signs!

4

Chapter 2: Identifying & Handling Codependency

We pursue relationships because they provide us with a sense of self-worth and fulfillment, while also allowing us to positively impact others. Interdependency, characterized by feeling connected to others, is a natural and beneficial state for human beings. It forms the foundation of thriving societies, enabling collaboration on projects and the nurturing of future generations.

Physical expressions of affection like hugging and touching, along with fostering strong emotional connections, elicit feelings of joy and enthusiasm, motivating us to seek further interactions with others. Essentially, human beings are inherently designed for relationships.

What constitutes codependency?

Unfortunately, many individuals enter romantic relationships without the readiness or capability to view their partner as an equal. Ideally, a relationship should facilitate the coming together of two distinct individuals to form a strong connection that honors each person's individuality. You should feel confident in your own identity and acknowledge your partner as an autonomous individual with their own needs, desires, and aspirations.

This might sound appealing, but achieving such a relationship demands a strong sense of self-worth and independence. However, many of us are raised in environments that do not foster healthy interdependence. Instead, we are taught that relationships where boundaries are blurred are normal. In a codependent relationship, you constantly feel as though your emotions and identity are intertwined with those of your partner.

Identifying codependency

If you're experiencing codependency, your approach to relating and communicating with others will exhibit distinct patterns. Here are some insightful questions for self-reflection:

1. Do you find yourself absorbing the moods of others? When a friend or partner appears upset or angry, do you also feel your own emotional state deteriorating? Is it challenging for you to maintain a sense of calm or happiness when someone else is distressed? Codependent individuals often struggle to connect with their own emotions, relying instead on others to dictate their feelings. They often take on the responsibility of

managing others' emotions. If you feel compelled to rectify someone else's negative mood, you may be exhibiting signs of codependency.
2. Do you second-guess your decisions and life choices when faced with disagreement? Codependency often manifests as indecisiveness and a willingness to alter plans based on others' opinions. Conflict avoidance is common, leading codependent individuals to prioritize harmony over asserting their own preferences.
3. Do you experience anxiety at the thought of someone leaving you? Fear of abandonment is a defining feature of codependency. The prospect of a relationship ending can evoke intense feelings of insecurity and distress.
4. Do you attempt to control your partner's behavior? While codependent individuals may rely on others for validation, they may also exert significant effort in trying to change them. This desire for control serves to create a sense of security within the relationship.
5. Do you struggle to differentiate between your partner's problems and your own? Assuming responsibility for solving all of your partner's issues can lead to overwhelming stress and neglect of your own needs. If you find yourself constantly preoccupied with your partner's challenges, you may be grappling with codependency.

Understanding the Causes of Codependency

Two primary factors contribute to the development of codependency. The first factor is rooted in childhood experiences. Individuals raised in tumultuous or unsafe home environments often adopt coping mechanisms to ensure their emotional survival. For instance, a child with abusive parents may learn to pacify them in hopes of averting further harm.

Since safety is a fundamental need, children will instinctively resort to any means necessary to attain it. However, when these coping strategies persist into adulthood, they can become problematic. For example, an individual who grew up in an abusive household may carry the belief that unless they maintain peace and harmony, catastrophic outcomes may ensue.

The second factor involves cultural influences, particularly prevalent in Western societies, that perpetuate codependent behaviors. Common phrases like "other half" or "better half" imply that entering a relationship will miraculously resolve all emotional and psychological issues. Such societal norms fail to promote healthy, independent relationships.

In healthy relationships, two autonomous individuals come together to form a mutually enriching bond. Conversely, codependent relationships lack this dynamic, as both parties rely heavily on each other for validation and guidance. Some codependent individuals seek direction from their partners on various aspects of life, including beliefs, behaviors, and interactions with others.

Effective Communication Techniques for Individuals

Struggling with Codependency If you find yourself identifying with traits of codependency, there's hope for change through dedication and time. Transforming your relationships starts with adopting new communication methods.

Firstly, acknowledge your own basic human needs. Codependent individuals often mask their true feelings in relationships, pretending everything is fine even when it's not. Embrace authenticity by engaging in genuine conversations and expressing your vulnerabilities.

Avoid the trap of expecting others to read your mind. In codependent relationships, individuals blur boundaries to the extent that they believe their thoughts and emotions are shared. However, this assumption leads to misunderstandings and disappointment. Instead, communicate openly about your desires and needs.

For instance, consider a scenario where Kelly, a codependent woman, anticipates Jim to intuitively know she wants a gold necklace for her birthday. When Jim chooses a different gift, confusion arises. In contrast, a non-codependent person would clearly communicate their preferences without relying on mind-reading.

Learn to evaluate advice independently. Codependent individuals often struggle to maintain their own values when faced with opposing opinions. Challenge assumptions and ask probing questions to gain a comprehensive understanding.

Furthermore, refrain from offering unsolicited advice. Respect others' autonomy by refraining from interference unless requested. While taking control may provide a sense of security, it impedes the development of balanced relationships founded on mutual respect and individual agency.

Challenge Assumptions: Individuals struggling with codependency often fear judgment because they automatically assume that any criticism directed at them is valid and that it reflects their inherent "badness," possibly leading to abandonment. However, neither of these assumptions holds true. Overcoming codependency involves questioning whether the judgments are objective or merely opinions. Developing self-esteem and a sense of identity reduces the significance of others' opinions.

Address Passive-Aggressive Behavior: Codependent individuals often suppress their true needs, pretending everything is fine while internally harboring resentment. However, this unresolved resentment eventually surfaces, leading to harmful passive-aggressive communication patterns. Instead, individuals should strive for assertive communication, expressing genuine thoughts and feelings rather than catering to perceived expectations.

Prioritize Individuals Over Outcomes: Codependency drains energy as individuals focus on controlling their partners rather than empathetically listening to their needs. Rather than engaging in authentic conversations, they fixate on achieving specific outcomes, treating their partners as pawns in a hypothetical game. Breaking free from codependency involves relinquishing the urge to control others and instead fostering mutually beneficial agreements through effective communication, active listening, and conflict resolution skills.

The Essential Asset for Individuals Struggling with Codependency.

The aforementioned strategies are crucial for fostering healthier relationships and shifting from codependency towards interdependency. However, there's a vital tool that hasn't been mentioned yet. Overcoming codependency hinges on establishing clear boundaries between yourself and others, delineating acceptable and unacceptable behaviors from those around you. In therapeutic contexts, this concept is known as "setting boundaries." Boundaries are indispensable; without them, fostering healthy relationships becomes nearly impossible.

When boundaries are absent, individuals often feel accountable not only for their own actions and emotions but also for those of others. Such is the significance of boundaries that the subsequent chapter is entirely dedicated to exploring this topic. Turn the page and discover how to assert yourself in any situation, learning the art of setting boundaries effectively.

5

Chapter 3: Setting & Defending Boundaries In A Relationship

A boundary serves as a psychological barrier, akin to a fence. Establishing a boundary means informing others that certain behaviors are unacceptable, and if they persist, there will be repercussions. Effectively setting and upholding boundaries relies on having strong self-esteem and proficient communication skills. Self-esteem enables you to determine what behaviors and individuals you will or will not accept in your life, while your communication abilities empower you to hold others accountable if they infringe upon your boundaries.

When individuals lack the knowledge of how to express their boundaries verbally, they resort to unhealthy methods. These may include yelling, screaming, or withdrawing. Needless to say, such approaches are detrimental to relationships. In this chapter, I will guide you on how to maintain your boundaries calmly and with dignity.

Why are boundaries crucial for healthy relationships?

For those unaccustomed to asserting themselves, the idea of boundaries might initially cause discomfort. People who habitually prioritize others' needs over their own may perceive setting personal boundaries as selfish, which is entirely unfounded. Surprisingly, establishing boundaries benefits not only oneself but also those in one's life. Generally, individuals respect those who steadfastly uphold their beliefs, exhibit consistent behavior, and recognize their own value. Whether raising children or managing others professionally, enforcing boundaries sets a positive example. While refining boundaries won't necessarily endear everyone to you, it does reduce susceptibility to bullies and negativity.

Selecting Your Boundaries Determining boundaries is a personal endeavor.

Each person possesses unique tastes, preferences, and personality traits. For instance, I'm comfortable listening to others' life stories and sharing personal details early in relationships, as it feels natural to me. However, some friends prefer to keep their personal lives private until trust has been established with a new acquaintance. My boundaries regarding personal information sharing are relatively relaxed; it takes considerable probing for me to halt inquiries. Conversely, my friends have stricter boundaries; they refrain from discussing health issues unless they've formed a bond with the other person, promptly signaling that the topic is off-limits if broached prematurely. Neither approach is inherently right or wrong. As long as one possesses the self-awareness to select boundaries that align with their needs and the ability to communicate these boundaries effectively, they will fare well.

If you're uncertain about your boundaries, consider the following:

Physical boundaries:

These pertain to physical closeness and contact. While some individuals may feel comfortable hugging friends and acquaintances, others prefer maintaining distance. Individuals with well-defined personal boundaries can deter inappropriate touching and make autonomous decisions regarding social interactions like kissing and hugging. Reflect on what situations make you uneasy and contemplate the boundaries you wish to establish. For example, you might decide not to hug someone unless they are a longstanding close friend. In this scenario, stating, "I reserve hugs for close acquaintances; being pressured into one is unacceptable to me," sets a clear boundary.

Emotional boundaries:

How much influence do you allow someone else's emotions to have on yours? Do you have set limits on how frequently others can confide in you? With robust emotional boundaries, you cease absorbing others' emotions and establish a clear distinction between yourself and them, thereby breaking free from codependency. If you realize that serving as an emotional dumping ground for others is affecting your well-being, it's time to establish boundaries. For instance, you might determine that you won't engage in negative conversations past 9 pm to ensure proper rest before work the next day. Setting a boundary like "I don't respond to non-emergency calls after 9 pm" would be appropriate in this context.

CHAPTER 3: SETTING & DEFENDING BOUNDARIES IN A RELATIONSHIP

Communication boundaries

This involve how others address you and the language they use. Examples include refusing to tolerate shouting or mocking. Upholding these boundaries shields you from manipulation, preventing emotional blackmail. Asserting that others' feelings are not your responsibility grants you emotional freedom, though it may unsettle them. Some boundaries may be flexible, like leaving if a friend abuses substances, while others are non-negotiable. It's crucial to communicate your limits comfortably.

Here are effective ways to express boundaries:

- Use "I" statements to express your perspective rather than passing judgment, reducing resistance.
- Avoid euphemisms; be direct about unacceptable behavior. For instance, say, "Your offensive language makes me uncomfortable; I won't tolerate it."
- Start with a positive statement if you believe the person meant well but crossed a boundary inadvertently. For example, acknowledge their caring intention before stating your discomfort with hugs.

Phrases to Establish Your Boundaries

Let's dive into the effective phrases that help define boundaries. Here's how to address someone who encroaches on your physical or emotional space:

- Utilize "I" statements: Express your viewpoint directly (e.g., "I need you to stop...") rather than judging the other person's actions or thoughts (e.g., "You always..."). This approach minimizes resistance since nobody can dispute your own thoughts and feelings.
- Avoid euphemisms: Be straightforward when setting boundaries; don't tiptoe around unacceptable behavior. For instance, if someone uses offensive language, explicitly state, "Your words are offensive and make

me uncomfortable. I refuse to tolerate it. If it persists, I will leave."
- Begin with a positive note if feasible: If you believe the person acted with good intentions but crossed a boundary unintentionally, starting with praise or acknowledgment can set a constructive tone. For instance, before explaining your discomfort with hugs, acknowledge their caring intent.

Adopt the Five-Step Framework:

Professional coach and author Kimberly Fulcher proposes a structured five-step method for expressing boundaries:

- Define the issue at hand.
- Clearly state what aspect of their behavior is unacceptable.
- Express how their actions impact you emotionally.
- Request a solution to prevent future boundary breaches.
- Communicate the consequences of disregarding your request.

For example, if a colleague repeatedly borrows your office equipment without permission, you should establish a firm boundary using the following format:

"I've noticed that you've been borrowing my equipment without asking for permission. This behavior is unacceptable as it disrupts my work. It leaves me feeling frustrated and anxious about meeting deadlines. Please ensure to seek permission before borrowing any equipment in the future. Failure to comply may result in me locking it away or escalating the issue formally."

Hone Your Conflict Resolution Skills:

Strengthening your ability to handle rejection, disagreements, and potential abandonment will empower you to assert your boundaries more effectively. Interacting with others becomes less daunting when you trust yourself to respond appropriately to their words and actions. Remember, it's crucial not to apologize for setting boundaries as they are essential for your mental well-being. Upholding your boundaries signifies self-respect, and if others struggle with that, it's their issue to address.

Align Actions with Words:

Consistency between your words and actions reinforces the importance of your boundaries. Demonstrating through your behavior that your boundaries matter is key to being taken seriously. For instance, if you ask your partner to share household responsibilities equally but continue to clean up after them, your actions contradict your words, undermining the integrity of your boundary.

Anticipate and Prepare for Challenges:

Proactively identify situations that make you uncomfortable and rehearse the language needed to assert your boundaries. Having a prepared response can be particularly helpful in scenarios where you feel pressured for an immediate answer. For example, when confronted with an unexpected question demanding an instant response, having a predetermined boundary statement such as "I need time to reflect on that and will get back to you within an hour" allows you to assert your need for space and time to consider your response.

Consistency Holds Key Importance.

Individuals with emotional intelligence typically honor the boundaries you set. However, it's evident that not everyone has fully developed this skill. Occasionally, you'll encounter individuals who attempt to disregard your boundaries. In such cases, there are only two effective solutions. Firstly, maintain firmness and consistency by reiterating your boundary statement, using a clear and assertive tone as needed. If despite your efforts, they persist in disregarding your boundaries, it's time to enact consequences. It's crucial to adhere to the consequences outlined in your initial boundary statement.

Failing to follow through might convey weakness to others.

Many of my clients find it challenging to establish boundaries. When I guide them through the five-step process, they often express hesitation or doubt, claiming they lack assertiveness. However, this is unfounded. Setting boundaries is a skill that anyone can develop with practice, albeit initially uncomfortable. It's undeniably a skill worth cultivating. By committing to applying the advice provided in this chapter, you'll soon experience more fulfilling relationships.

6

Chapter 4: Defining A Relationship

Transitioning from casual dating to a committed relationship is a pivotal stage in any romantic journey. While some couples seamlessly evolve into this phase without needing to explicitly discuss it, many find themselves uncertain about their partner's intentions and desires. However, with proper preparation and readiness for various outcomes, you can navigate this conversation with grace and composure.

The Typical Progression of Dating Scenarios:

Does this narrative resonate with your own experiences? You meet someone intriguing, go on a series of dates, and perhaps intimacy follows suit. In due time, you start contemplating the idea of formalizing the relationship, only to find yourself grappling with uncertainties regarding your partner's stance on the matter.

It's remarkable how swiftly the desire to clarify the relationship's trajectory intensifies as time passes. At this juncture, you face a critical decision: continue in limbo, hoping your partner initiates the discussion, or take the proactive approach of initiating "the talk."

Opting to prolong the ambiguity often leads to escalating anxiety and overthinking. Each passing day only fuels your curiosity about your partner's thoughts and intentions, potentially altering your behavior and demeanor, which can perplex your partner.

Conversely, directly addressing the topic with your partner offers transparency and authenticity. With careful planning, you can broach the subject candidly, increasing the likelihood of obtaining the clarity you seek.

Ideally, a strong emotional connection fosters open communication, allowing for straightforward questioning. However, in certain circumstances, a gentler or more casual approach may be preferable.

The Challenge of Initiating "The Talk"

Engaging in the discussion about the status of a relationship can be daunting for several reasons:

We Fear Appearing Desperate:

Societal pressures compel both genders to avoid coming across as needy or desperate. While there's merit in maintaining independence and confidence, this can lead to a stalemate when both individuals are intent on playing it cool.

Consequently, ambiguity ensues, leaving both parties perplexed about the relationship's direction.

We Resist Facing Unpleasant Realities:

At times, our instincts may signal that the other person isn't genuinely interested, but we prefer to remain in denial rather than confront the truth. The fear of rejection often drives us to evade confronting the situation head-on. However, delaying the inevitable discussion only prolongs the uncertainty.

Ignoring Intuition Leads to Regrets:

Personal anecdotes often highlight the consequences of ignoring intuition. For instance, recalling an encounter with someone named Zoe, who exhibited subtle signs of disinterest, despite enjoyable dates. Despite warnings from a friend, the narrator proceeded with high hopes, only to face disappointment when Zoe revealed she wasn't seeking a relationship.

The Importance of Trusting Intuition:

This experience underscores the significance of trusting one's instincts. While the outcome was painful, it served as a valuable lesson. However, the narrator acknowledges that the situation could have been more distressing if they had avoided initiating the conversation altogether, potentially investing months in a futile pursuit.

Strategies for Initiating "The Talk"

Preparing to broach the topic of defining the relationship requires careful consideration. Whether you opt for a direct approach or a more subtle method, here are some key pointers to bear in mind:

Face-to-Face Communication is Vital:

Avoid the temptation to address such a significant conversation through digital means like email or text, or even via phone call. Being able to observe their body language and facial expressions is crucial for effective communication. Despite the apprehension, it's imperative to adhere to this rule.

Ease into the Conversation:

Rather than abruptly posing a formal question, initiate the discussion by sharing your observations or experiences from your time together. Conclude your statement with an open-ended question that invites their input. For instance: "After spending considerable time together recently, it feels like our connection is evolving. What are your thoughts on where this is headed?" "I've genuinely enjoyed our time together, and I'm interested in exploring an exclusive dating arrangement. Would you be open to that?"

Trust Their Response:

While it's natural to rehearse what you'll say, remember that if they reciprocate your feelings, they'll likely welcome the opportunity to express their sentiments. Conversely, they might feel apprehensive about broaching the topic themselves, even if they desire a deeper relationship. Hence, keeping the conversation concise and to the point is essential to prevent unnecessary suspense.

Avoid Preemptive Warnings:

Refrain from forewarning them about the impending discussion, as this might induce defensiveness and create an imbalance of power. Providing no advance notice fosters fairness and trust by preventing undue anticipation.

Practice Active Listening:

If they attempt to interject during the conversation, allow them to express themselves fully. They may have contemplated the discussion in advance and have prepared responses. Hence, attentive listening is crucial for fostering open communication and understanding.

Having "the talk" too early in a relationship can often raise concerns for both parties. Discussing relationship status within the initial weeks is generally ill-advised. It's crucial to allow time for getting to know each other before delving into such topics. Adhering to the three-month guideline usually proves beneficial in most cases.

Understanding your own desires and requirements is paramount. Whether it's seeking a committed, monogamous relationship or opting for an open arrangement, everyone has distinct preferences. It's imperative to recognize and respect your own needs without succumbing to pressure to compromise on them merely to gain acceptance from someone else.

Never settle for less than what aligns with your relationship objectives, regardless of how strong your feelings may be. If a potential partner's offerings fail to meet your standards, it's essential to value yourself enough to seek compatibility elsewhere.

Prepare yourself for the possibility of receiving an unfavorable response. Having a response plan in place can provide a moment of respite in case of emotional distress: "It's okay, I just need a moment, don't worry." "I'll be fine, I'm just a bit disappointed." "Can I step outside for a moment? I'll be right back."

Express gratitude for their honesty once you've regained composure. While rejection may sting, clarity about where you stand is valuable. A rejection does not diminish your worth or courage in pursuing romantic connections; it merely demonstrates your willingness to take emotional risks.

Ensure that the conversation occurs in a neutral setting where either party can easily depart if necessary. Avoid discussing such matters late at night or in overly intimate settings, opting instead for places like parks or quiet coffee shops.

If your partner seems unsure or hesitant, grant them additional time to contemplate their feelings. However, it's crucial to establish a timeframe for revisiting the conversation to prevent prolonged uncertainty.

Following a rejection, it's advisable to refrain from immediate contact for a period. Transitioning directly from romantic interest to friendship can be emotionally taxing and is generally not advisable.

Certainly, there's a possibility of building a friendship down the road, but it's contingent on being able to envision them with another person without feeling distraught. There's no need to engage in manipulative tactics. Instead, express your emotions honestly and make it clear that being friends isn't feasible for you in the near future.

It's important to be aware that some individuals may feel remorseful for causing you distress and may urge maintaining contact under the guise of friendship. However, as previously explained, this arrangement is unlikely to be sustainable. Prioritize your emotional well-being and uphold your boundaries.

7

Chapter 5: Your Partner's Most Important Need, & How To Meet It

Relationships come to an end due to various reasons, but there's a significant risk factor often overlooked. While trust issues, conflicting worldviews, and the stress of major life events are known to strain relationships, the most damaging risk is often the threat of abandonment. When either partner suggests leaving the relationship, it strains the bond between them. This chapter will delve into the reasons behind this phenomenon, exploring why the fear of abandonment is such a sensitive issue for many individuals and how trust can be nurtured. Ultimately, trust and security are paramount for a healthy relationship, and neglecting them can have dire consequences.

The Inevitability of Conflict

Some individuals mistakenly interpret disagreements within a relationship as a sign of inherent incompatibility. However, it's not the presence of arguments that necessarily drives a couple apart, but rather the sense of security within the relationship. Additionally, we need to reassess the notion that conflicts solely arise from clashes in beliefs and ideas.

While it's true that disagreements often stem from differing viewpoints, Stan Tatkin, a specialist in communication and neuroscience, suggests that delving into neurobiology can shed light on why certain relationships deteriorate. Instead of solely focusing on verbal or behavioral interactions with our partners, it's crucial to consider the workings of our primal, or "animal," brains during social encounters.

Understanding the basic functions of the brain doesn't require expertise in neuroscience. Essentially, the "higher" brain regions, located towards the front and visible on the surface, govern conscious thought processes, enabling us to rationalize and make deliberate decisions. Conversely, the remaining portions of the brain, often dubbed the "lower" or "primitive" brain, operate on autopilot and serve as our threat detection system, allowing us to react swiftly to potential dangers, whether physical, emotional, or psychological.

Importantly, the lower brain automates habitual behaviors and routines, forming procedural memories through repetitive actions like playing an instrument or driving. Consequently, when engaging in such tasks, the higher brain can relinquish control, allowing for efficient and instinctive responses without conscious deliberation.

Love: From Intense Focus to Routine

When initially meeting and dating someone, your conscious mind meticulously scrutinizes their words, actions, and the potential compatibility between you two. Your higher brain becomes fixated on this individual, striving to explore every facet of their personality. Hormonal shifts in the brain and body actively support this infatuated state.

For instance, serotonin levels decrease, prompting a desire to seek happiness from the other person. Testosterone levels also fluctuate; typically, a man's testosterone levels decrease while a woman's increase when experiencing love. Although the precise reasons for these changes remain unclear, it's evident that love profoundly alters our body chemistry.

Nevertheless, even the most intense infatuations inevitably wane over time. As familiarity grows within the relationship, excitement diminishes, as we start to settle into a comfortable routine with our partner.

This transition into comfort is natural and necessary; perpetual romantic obsession would hinder productivity and other aspects of life. However, the problem arises when partners begin to take each other for granted, assuming they can effortlessly decipher each other's thoughts and feelings. Consequently, the relationship shifts into autopilot mode, leading to decreased attentiveness towards each other's words and actions.

The consequence? Misunderstandings and rapid escalations in arguments, familiar to anyone who's been caught in a sudden, intense dispute. Long-term couples often resort to phrases like "You always..." or "You never...", which exacerbate tensions and set the stage for further conflict.

Understanding Why Threats of Abandonment Arise in Couples

During conflicts, both the mind and body become hypersensitive to potential threats. The lower brain activates, releasing adrenaline and cortisol, triggering the instinctual "fight or flight" response. In such moments, rational thinking becomes challenging, and emotions overshadow the original cause of the argument. Tensions escalate, leading to impulsive threats such as "I've had enough! I'm done with this relationship!" or "Maybe I'll just leave you alone!"

As emotions intensify, both parties may resort to shouting and screaming as their nervous systems go into overdrive. While making such threats may provide temporary relief, the long-term consequences can be detrimental to the relationship. Threats erode trust, making it difficult to believe in a partner who repeatedly considers leaving. Moreover, it sets a precedent for future conflicts, as the threatened party may hesitate to confide in their partner, fearing abandonment will be used against them in future disputes.

The Significance of Threats of Abandonment

You might be curious about why we react strongly to the mere suggestion of a partner leaving us. The roots of this sensitivity lie in our early experiences with attachment and abandonment. During infancy, we rely entirely on caregivers, typically our mothers, for our basic needs. If these caregivers fail to consistently provide love and care, we develop profound anxiety because, at a primal level, we understand that survival depends on their support.

Even as adults capable of self-care, we retain a fundamental need for secure and stable relationships. In healthy parent-child dynamics, a secure attachment forms, wherein the child feels a deep connection with the parent and trusts their love and return. Conversely, a lack of consistent love and attention leads to relationship anxiety, termed an "insecure attachment style" by psychologists.

While everyone fears abandonment to some extent, those with an insecure attachment style struggle immensely with trust, often anticipating eventual abandonment from everyone. Consequently, threats of abandonment hit them particularly hard.

Research indicates that the quality of parental relationships during youth significantly influences attitudes towards romantic relationships in adulthood. Individuals who felt secure and loved as children exhibit more confidence in their adult relationships. Conversely, those with tumultuous parental relationships tend to fear abandonment, seeking validation from their partners. They also experience heightened negative emotions and exhibit lower levels of commitment.

This research underscores that the need for safety and security remains ingrained in our brains, driven by primitive instincts and early habits. Even in adulthood, we yearn for assurance that our loved ones won't suddenly depart, a concern amplified for those with unstable early caregiver relationships. Building trust and stability in relationships significantly increases the likelihood of their endurance.

Fostering Trust and Stability in Your Relationship

Avoid Using Threats of Leaving for Control: It may be tempting to employ threats to gain control, especially if you know your partner fears abandonment, a common concern for many. However, using threats to evade discussions or coerce compliance is detrimental in the long run. While it might yield short-term results, your partner will grow weary of this manipulation tactic. If you notice your partner resorting to such threats, it's crucial to establish boundaries and communicate that this behavior is unacceptable.

Engage in Face-to-Face Communication: Effective communication relies heavily on eye contact and facial expressions. Arguments should be addressed directly, avoiding discussions over the phone, via text, or while sitting side by side. Wait until you can engage face to face to address sensitive issues. Face-to-face contact fosters trust, as it allows for better understanding and connection through eye contact.

Pause Before Reacting to Threats of Leaving: Rather than immediately reacting with your own threats or escalating the situation, break the cycle by taking a different approach. Change your physical position, take a deep breath, and request a moment to gather your thoughts. Seek to understand your partner's perspective by asking clarifying questions. Recognize that threats often arise when the lower brain is in control, signaling the need to pause and revisit the discussion later.

Consider Your Partner's Attachment Style: People develop different attachment styles based on their early experiences. Some may require reassurance periodically, especially during tense moments, while others may need less frequent reminders of love and commitment. Understand your partner's attachment style and tailor your responses accordingly, offering support and reassurance as needed.

Recognize the Importance of Equality and Trust: Even the most confident individuals desire validation and reassurance in their relationships. Mutual trust and equality form the foundation of strong relationships. In the following chapter, additional strategies will be explored to help both partners recognize each other as equals.

8

Chapter 6: How To Make Assertive Communication Work In Your Relationships

Considering your interest in communication and relationship skills, it's likely that you're familiar with the various communication styles prevalent in our interactions.

Passive Communication: Passive communicators tend to withhold their thoughts and emotions, prioritizing the needs of others over their own. Often perceived as pushovers, they may struggle to assert themselves.

Aggressive Communication: Individuals with an aggressive communication style prioritize their own needs without regard for others, often coming across as domineering or confrontational. While they may achieve their goals more easily, they risk being labeled as bullies.

Passive-Aggressive Communication: This style involves suppressing true feelings and expressing them indirectly, often through subtle actions or behaviors. For instance, agreeing to a task begrudgingly and then performing it poorly as a form of protest.

Assertive Communication: Assertive communicators strike a balance between their own needs and those of others. They are adept at compromise, handle difficult situations calmly, and express themselves confidently and directly.

Clearly, assertive communication stands out as the most effective and constructive style. Assertive individuals demonstrate respect for themselves and others, maintain confidence, and avoid engaging in manipulative behaviors.

The Five-Step Approach

Here's a practical five-step approach to effectively communicate assertively with your partner, applicable not only in romantic relationships but also with friends, family, and colleagues. This straightforward process facilitates the sharing of feelings, reduces conflict, and fosters healthy collaboration.

Step 1:

Begin by articulating your thoughts on the issue using factual and concise statements, avoiding excessive emotional expression. While emotions are valid, becoming too agitated or upset can trigger defensiveness in the other person, hindering receptiveness. Focus on one issue at a time and ensure clarity by checking if your partner comprehends your message through questions like "Do you understand what I mean?" or "Would you like me to rephrase that?"

Step 2:

Extend the respect you desire by refraining from interruptions and summarizing the other person's perspective. Reiterating their viewpoint with statements such as "So, you believe X because of Y, correct?" affirms understanding and encourages open dialogue.

If the individual seems hesitant to engage, employ questioning techniques to prompt discussion. Begin with closed or low-effort questions like "Do you agree with doing X?" or "Which event do you prefer, A or B?" to ease them into conversation. Be patient, especially with insecure or passive communicators, allowing them ample time to gather their thoughts fosters trust and facilitates smoother interactions over time.

Conversely, when faced with someone utilizing an aggressive communication style, establish boundaries to prevent dominance. Aggressive individuals may perceive passivity as an invitation to exert control, so maintaining assertiveness and clarity in communication is essential for setting and maintaining boundaries.

Utilize your boundaries to outline the repercussions of aggressive behavior, and be prepared to enforce them when necessary. Consider employing the following boundaries when confronted with an aggressive communicator:

"It's unacceptable for you to raise your voice at me. It makes me uncomfortable. If you can't communicate calmly, I will terminate this conversation."

"I won't tolerate insults. They make me feel diminished. Unless you stop insulting me immediately, I will take formal action."

"I refuse to entertain baseless criticisms during this discussion. If you can't stay on topic, I will leave."

When dealing with aggressive communicators, focus on proactive responses rather than reacting defensively. Instead of engaging in a tit-for-tat exchange of criticisms, propose potential solutions. Demonstrating your commitment to maintaining boundaries can earn you respect from aggressive individuals.

Avoid trying to appease them by empathizing with their anger or claiming to understand their perspective. They are likely to dismiss such attempts. Similarly, when faced with passive-aggressive behavior, remain composed and resist being drawn into their games.

Passive-aggressive individuals exhibit subtle signs such as insincere body language, sarcasm, evasion of questions, giving the silent treatment, and spreading negative rumors. They seek to provoke reactions without directly confronting issues. Treat them with patience, akin to dealing with an immature teenager, and avoid reinforcing their behavior by not giving undue attention to their antics. Stick to factual communication and refrain from rewarding their passive-aggressive actions with attention.

Step 3

Once both parties have expressed their perspectives, the focus shifts to conflict resolution and finding common ground through compromise. A constructive starting point is to inquire, "What aspects can we find agreement on?" Each individual will have their own needs and concerns, even in seemingly trivial situations.

Consider a scenario where a couple disagrees on vacation spending - one prefers a budget-friendly trip while the other desires an extravagant cruise. Despite differing preferences, they may share the desire for quality time together, creating lasting memories, and enjoying a break from work.

Identifying areas of agreement fosters trust and openness, making it easier for both parties to listen to each other's concerns. Discussions can then delve into fears, such as financial insecurity or relationship stagnation. Questions like "What do you need in this situation?" and "What worries you about this?" facilitate uncovering underlying fears and needs.

By prioritizing empathy and understanding, couples pave the way for mutually beneficial solutions. Recognizing and addressing each other's fears and needs forms a solid foundation for compromise.

For instance, after acknowledging the shared desire for enjoyable experiences and relaxation, along with the partner's aspiration for a unique trip, they could brainstorm cost-effective yet adventurous vacation ideas together. Turning the planning process into a fun challenge encourages creativity and collaboration, ultimately leading to a vacation plan that satisfies both parties within an agreed budget.

Step 4

Understanding What to Do When Consensus Isn't Achieved

Occasionally, you'll encounter situations where reaching an agreement seems impossible. This typically occurs when individuals hold deeply held beliefs or when their preferences are non-negotiable.

For instance, suppose you wish to adopt a child while your partner insists on having a biological child. In such cases, if neither party is willing to reconsider their stance, there's little room for compromise.

In such no-win scenarios, it's crucial to avoid resorting to aggression or passivity. It's not always about one person winning and the other losing. Recognizing and respecting each other's differing viewpoints doesn't imply agreement; it signifies emotional maturity and respect for individual autonomy.

Be open to the possibility of agreeing to disagree, understanding that discomfort or emotional distress may arise. Remember, differing opinions don't equate to moral superiority or inferiority. Emotionally mature individuals acknowledge that while agreement and compromise are beneficial, some situations may lead to deadlocks.

Step 5

Reflect on Your Internal Dialogue

When faced with disagreement, it's crucial to focus on what you can control: your own reactions and mindset. While you can't dictate others' thoughts or actions, you hold the power to choose how their opinions affect you.

Accept that not everyone will see eye-to-eye with you, and that's perfectly acceptable. Ensure you aren't harboring any resentment. If negative thoughts like "Nothing ever goes my way" or "Life is against me" arise, it's vital to shift your mindset before progressing.

Addressing your inner dialogue is paramount as it significantly influences your mood. Unaddressed negative thoughts can permeate your entire perspective on life. Research indicates that those prone to negative thinking are at risk of depression and often remain trapped in a cycle of negativity. Acknowledge these thoughts but challenge them; don't allow them to dominate your mindset.

The most effective method to counter these negative thoughts is to identify at least three pieces of evidence that refute them. If feasible, jot them down for reference.

For example, if you're feeling like nothing ever goes your way, recall three instances of good fortune you've encountered in the past year. Practicing gratitude can significantly alter your perspective.

Additionally, it's essential to devise a plan that accommodates your own needs to the best extent possible. In the aforementioned scenario, where there's a stark difference between your desire to adopt and your partner's preference for a biological child, options may seem limited. However, even in challenging circumstances, there are choices available. You could opt to remain childless, end the relationship to find a more compatible partner, or channel your nurturing instincts into a child-centered career.

Maintaining peace with reality, accepting the situation as it is, and refraining from dwelling on alternative outcomes are crucial for relationship stability. Seeking guidance from a counselor may be beneficial if necessary, as harboring resentment and dissatisfaction can not only impact your well-being but also harm your relationship.

In certain cases, meaningful dialogue may seem unattainable between two individuals. In the subsequent chapter, strategies for handling toxic situations, which pose a threat to mental health if left unaddressed, will be discussed.

9

Chapter 7: How to Identify & Handle Verbal Abuse

When discussing abuse, many people immediately associate it with physical violence. However, what about forms of abuse that don't involve bodily harm? Unfortunately, there's a common misconception that as long as someone isn't physically injuring you, they aren't an abuser. This misunderstanding can trap individuals in abusive relationships because they fail to recognize that verbal abuse is not acceptable.

CHAPTER 7: HOW TO IDENTIFY & HANDLE VERBAL ABUSE

While physical abuse is typically straightforward to identify—either there is force used against you or there isn't—verbal abuse presents a more complex picture. In this chapter, I'll provide a brief overview of verbal abuse, how to identify it, why it's detrimental to relationships, and how to address it.

Verbal abuse can affect anyone regardless of gender, sexual orientation, age, or relationship status. Although I'll primarily address verbal abuse within romantic partnerships, much of the advice in this chapter applies to abusive friendships or family dynamics. Ending a relationship isn't always necessary when dealing with verbal abuse, but it's crucial to equip yourself with knowledge before making any decisions, especially for your mental well-being.

Verbal abuse must be taken seriously as it can lead to depression, anxiety, low self-esteem, and social withdrawal. Moreover, it's not uncommon for verbal abuse to escalate into physical violence.

What constitutes verbal abuse?

Verbal abuse occurs when an individual intentionally communicates in a manner that inflicts emotional harm upon you. There are two primary aspects to verbal abuse: the content of what is said and the manner in which it is conveyed. Name-calling stands out as one of the most evident forms of verbal abuse. In adult relationships, there is no valid excuse for such behavior, as it serves no constructive purpose and is employed as a means to intimidate or silence the other party. If someone directs derogatory language at you, purposely provokes you, or otherwise makes you feel distressed through their words or tone, they are engaging in verbal abuse.

Other manifestations of verbal abuse encompass the following behaviors:

- *Disparaging someone else's viewpoints:*

While it's acceptable to hold differing opinions, criticizing someone's views without valid reason and using excessively harsh language (like labeling an opinion as "stupid" without cause) constitutes abusive behavior.

- *Gaslighting:*

This form of abuse aims to manipulate a victim's perception of reality, leading them to doubt their own memories or sanity. For instance, an abuser might falsely claim that the victim forgot a past event to undermine their confidence.

- *Blaming:*

Verbal abusers often deflect responsibility for their actions onto their victims, inducing guilt or compliance to avoid further conflict.

- *Excessive judgment or criticism:*

Verbal abusers employ harsh judgments and criticisms to intimidate others, attempting to establish dominance by presenting their opinions as absolute truths.

- *Deliberate withholding:*

While privacy is important, verbal abusers may exploit withholding tactics to keep their partners anxious or uncertain, thereby exerting control.

- *Trivializing:*

This involves diminishing a partner's achievements, social skills, or efforts in the relationship, gradually eroding their self-esteem. For example, an abuser might belittle their partner's attention or care, despite evidence to the contrary.

CHAPTER 7: HOW TO IDENTIFY & HANDLE VERBAL ABUSE

Regrettably, I've observed a similar type of verbal abuse within my own family dynamics. My maternal aunt, who is now divorced, was once married to a man notorious for belittling her accomplishments. I vividly recall an instance from my childhood when she secured a significant job at a legal firm after years of striving for a paralegal position.

Upon sharing this exciting news with her husband, his response was anything but congratulatory. Instead, he gazed at her for a moment, shrugged, and remarked, "That office will be full of young people just starting out in their careers. Won't that make you feel a bit old?" His lack of acknowledgment left my aunt feeling self-conscious about her age for weeks afterward, highlighting the profound impact of verbal abuse.

Another common tactic of abusers is denial, where they conveniently forget or outright deny their hurtful words and actions, leaving the victim disoriented and questioning their own reality—a classic form of gaslighting. Conversely, some abusers may feign remorse and offer insincere apologies, promising never to repeat their behavior, only for the cycle to inevitably recommence, whether after a few days or several months, perpetuating what's known as the "cycle of abuse."

What unites these forms of abuse is their shared objective of dominating the victim by eroding their confidence, whether overtly acknowledged or not. Various theories attempt to explain why individuals become verbally abusive, citing difficulties in emotion regulation or past experiences of childhood abuse as contributing factors. Regardless, my focus in this chapter is on providing practical strategies to cope with verbal abuse rather than delving into the ultimate explanation.

Techniques for managing verbal abuse.

Document conversations: Conceal a recording device discreetly within the vicinity where verbal abuse typically unfolds, or utilize your phone to record interactions with your partner. Reviewing past conversations can provide clarity by identifying recurring patterns of abuse, offering a crucial reality check. Additionally, these recordings serve as evidence to counter denial or false accusations, aiding in therapy sessions or legal proceedings.

Maintain a chronicle of significant occurrences: In conjunction with recordings, maintain a written record of instances of abuse, including dates, times, and contextual details. While recordings capture verbal exchanges, a diary can document the events leading up to the abuse. Ensure the secrecy of your diary by keeping it hidden or utilizing password-protected digital formats.

Adapt your internal dialogue: Verbal abuse becomes particularly distressing when the victim internalizes the abuser's words. Recognizing that you cannot control the abuser's actions but can manage your own responses is crucial. Reframe the abuser's remarks within your mind as attempts to manipulate rather than truths. For instance, if they insult your appearance, consciously remind yourself that their words stem from a desire to assert dominance rather than reflecting reality. While this strategy may not halt the abuse immediately, it can serve as a temporary shield to preserve your self-worth.

If safe, uphold your boundaries: While defending your boundaries might provoke a verbal abuser or escalate to physical violence, it's crucial to communicate that you won't tolerate their actions. For detailed guidance on this, revisit the chapter dedicated to establishing and maintaining boundaries. Avoid attempting to rationalize with a verbal abuser, as they seek dominance rather than constructive dialogue.

Gain perspective from a trusted source: Share your experiences with a reliable friend or family member to obtain an objective viewpoint. Someone outside your relationship can offer insight into whether your encounters are typical. However, be cautious as not everyone comprehends the severity of verbal abuse, and some may downplay your ordeal. Seek support from those who validate your experiences.

CHAPTER 7: HOW TO IDENTIFY & HANDLE VERBAL ABUSE

Cultivate self-assurance independent of external validation: Strengthen your self-esteem to reduce vulnerability to your partner's hurtful remarks. Invest your energy in nurturing relationships, expanding your social circle, and advancing professionally.

Consider therapy: While verbal abusers often resist seeking help, therapy can benefit victims in understanding and coping with their situation. A therapist specializing in abuse can offer guidance and support. If feasible, encourage your partner to participate in couples therapy to address relationship issues.

Refrain from retaliating with abuse: Despite feeling provoked, responding with insults only perpetuates the cycle of abuse and undermines your values. Engaging in abusive behavior, even in self-defense, provides ammunition for your abuser to discredit you in future conflicts.

Understanding why a victim stays with an abuser

This is often perplexing to those unfamiliar with abusive relationships. However, the reality is far from straightforward. Some victims rely on their abusers for financial stability, shelter, or other essential support systems. Others remain in denial, holding onto hope that the abuser will change, although this usually requires therapy and a genuine commitment to self-improvement.

Many abusers initially treat their victims with kindness, luring them into a relationship where love blossoms. When the abuse eventually surfaces, victims struggle to break free. Gradually, they normalize the abuse, forgetting what life was like before the emotional turmoil began. If they entered the relationship with low self-esteem, they may even believe they deserve the treatment they receive. Additionally, because abuse often occurs in cycles, victims may cling to the hope that the abuser's "good" behavior will persist indefinitely. It may take years before they confront the harsh reality and realize that change is unlikely without significant intervention.

If you're in need of support or guidance to escape an abusive relationship, several resources are available to help you make informed decisions. The National Domestic Violence Hotline provides round-the-clock support via phone and online services. Similarly, the Women's Health website offers valuable resources for women seeking assistance.

While abusive individuals undoubtedly exert a negative influence, it's essential to distinguish between general negativity and abusive behavior. In the subsequent chapter, I'll explore strategies for dealing with everyday negativity.

10

Chapter 8: Dealing with Negative People

In the previous section, we delved into the topic of verbal abuse. But what about individuals who, while not necessarily abusive, have a knack for bringing down the mood? In this segment, I'll outline how to identify negative people—often less obvious than one might assume—and provide techniques for maintaining positivity, even in their presence.

Negative individuals come in various forms:

- **Straight-up negative individuals**: These are the ones who consistently see the glass as half empty. They drain the energy from any room they enter, prompting others to steer clear.
- **Martyrs**: Initially, martyrs appear selfless, always prioritizing others' needs. However, they eventually lament their sacrifices, seeking sympathy and validation for their self-imposed burdens.
- **Relentless judges**: Everyone forms opinions, but judgmental individuals vocalize theirs incessantly. They highlight flaws in others without restraint, fostering an atmosphere of criticism.
- **Distractors**: Distractors may not overtly express negativity, making them harder to detect. Instead, they consume your time and attention, hindering your progress toward personal goals.

Dealing with negative people follows a two-step approach:

Firstly, recognize that limiting interaction with them is often the most effective strategy. While you may empathize with their struggles, assuming the role of their therapist is neither beneficial nor your responsibility.

Secondly, for those unavoidable negative individuals, adopt a proactive mindset and employ communication tactics to neutralize their negativity, allowing you to maintain your peace of mind and focus on your own goals.

Step One: Adjust Your Perspective.

If you find yourself unable to influence someone else's behavior, don't lose hope. You always have the power to control how you respond to a given situation. Reflect on your recent encounter with a negative individual. Allow me to share a personal experience from a few months back involving my neighbor. Let's call her "Sally": ME: "Good morning, Sally! Lovely weather we're having, isn't it?" SALLY: "Unusually hot for March, and no rain in sight for weeks!" ME: "Indeed, quite warm for this time of year." SALLY: "That's probably why the grass looks dreadful. You're off to an early start today." ME: "Yes, I have a meeting with a new client. Excited about the opportunity!" SALLY: "You seem to work a lot. I don't understand this modern obsession with constant work. I bet you're exhausted by the end of the week."

At this point, I politely wrapped up the conversation and headed to my car, feeling less than thrilled about the morning encounter. Does this scenario sound familiar? Many of us have encountered similar situations! While I can't entirely avoid interacting with Sally, as our paths cross multiple times a day, I aim to maintain a positive relationship with all my neighbors. Fortunately, I've developed strategies to prevent her negative demeanor from affecting my mood. Here are the techniques I employ in such circumstances.

Changing Your Mindset.

Consider the following statements. Can you detect the subtle contrast? "Sally is a negative person." "Sally has a lot of negativity." In the first statement, we imply that Sally fundamentally embodies negativity. This judgment may be justified if our interactions with her consistently reveal a negative demeanor. Our perceptions are shaped by our experiences. However, I find the second statement intriguing. While not the most eloquent phrasing, it proves valuable for maintaining a positive outlook amid someone else's grievances and complaints. The crucial term here is "has." Sally possesses her negativity; it belongs solely to her. It doesn't belong to me, her spouse, or anyone else. I am not obligated to embrace it.

Realizing that I can allow someone to take ownership of their attitude, and I can choose whether to engage with it or disregard it, has diminished the impact of negative individuals on me. Remember:

- Just as others have no right to dictate your mood, you lack the right to control theirs.

- When confronted with negativity, you needn't internalize it.
- You are not obligated to stoop to someone else's level. You are not responsible for alleviating their distress or lifting their spirits.
- Allowing your emotions to be swayed by someone else's mood isn't healthy; it signifies codependency, which is detrimental to relationships.
- Anyone presuming that your role in a relationship involves listening to their complaints endlessly or being their constant source of cheer is detrimental. They will deplete your energy rapidly.

Utilizing Hanlon's Razor to Handle Critical Individuals.

Have you ever been confronted with a particularly foolish or toxic opinion that ruined your mood for the entire day? I certainly have! Thankfully, I stumbled upon an insightful quote that revolutionized how I approach judgmental individuals.

While you're likely familiar with Occam's Razor, which suggests that the simplest explanation is often the correct one, have you heard of Hanlon's Razor? Coined by author Robert J. Hanlon, it goes like this:

"Never attribute to malice that which can be adequately explained by stupidity."

Hanlon's Razor serves as a valuable reminder that most of the negative and judgmental individuals I encounter aren't necessarily targeting me personally. Instead, they may be making ignorant or uninformed remarks due to their own lack of knowledge or understanding. I can't fault them for that; in many cases, they may simply be unaware.

And even if they are aware, I find it more beneficial to assume they are ignorant rather than malicious, as it helps me maintain my composure. If someone wishes to engage in a constructive debate, I'm open to it. However, I generally choose to brush off ignorant comments.

In fact, I've turned it into a bit of a game! Whenever I encounter negative or judgmental remarks, I mentally chant "Hanlon! Hanlon!" This not only brings a smile to my face but also helps me overlook their foolish statements.

When dealing with someone like Sally, for instance, I remind myself that her lack of experience in the workforce (as she is a homemaker while her husband is the primary breadwinner) likely means she has limited insight into careers and workplace dynamics.

Step Two: Employing Three Phrases to Counter Negativity

There isn't a universal set of words that will effectively address every negative individual. The most suitable approach will vary based on your relationship with the person, the available time, and the root cause of their negativity.

While it's natural to adopt a more empathetic stance, especially in romantic relationships, it doesn't mean you must endure endless hours of their negativity.

Here are three helpful phrases to use when dealing with someone who is complaining without purpose:

- "That's unfortunate. Did anything positive come out of it?": This approach catches negative individuals off guard. It compels them to acknowledge any positive aspects of the situation or, if there are none, it provides an opportunity to gracefully shift the conversation away from negativity.
- "I hear what you're saying, but talking like this isn't going to change the situation. I'm going to suggest that we talk about something else.": This statement validates the other person's feelings while gently guiding the discussion toward a more positive topic.
- "What do you need me to do?": This phrase offers a less confrontational alternative to "Well, what can I do about it?" yet serves the same purpose.

It prompts the other person to pause their venting and focus on whether the problem can be resolved and, if so, how.

By using these phrases, the complainer will either realize the futility of their complaints or shift the conversation toward constructive problem-solving if assistance is genuinely needed.

Handling Pessimistic Individuals

Resist the temptation to engage in arguments with those who consistently make negative forecasts just for the sake of it. They're not interested in a genuine discussion about the topic at hand. If they were, they would have provided rationale for their stance and sought your input. When someone predicts doom simply to dampen spirits, it's wise to tactfully put a stop to it.

Depending on your relationship with the individual and their receptiveness to rejection, consider using these tactics. Note that they are diversionary strategies. Ignoring the person might come across as impolite, while engaging with them will only drag you into their negative spiral.

- "We'll wait and see. Anyway…"
- "Thank you for your input. So anyway…"
- "I'll consider that. Meanwhile…"
- "Having another perspective is valuable. Now, let's focus on…"
- "It's interesting how perspectives can differ! Anyway, as I was saying…"
- "That's a possibility! But let's shift to a more positive topic…"

Maintain Your Personal Boundaries

If you've been following along, you'll know that I advocate for setting boundaries as a crucial aspect of relationships. Boundaries prove invaluable when dealing with negative individuals. Consider their negativity as a behavior that you don't have to endure. Just as you would assert your boundaries if someone insulted you or invaded your personal space, you can apply the same principles when faced with someone's negativity.

Let's explore how this concept plays out in real-life scenarios. Recently, at a family gathering, I found myself seated next to my cousin at the dinner table. What ensued is a firsthand example that perfectly illustrates this point.

Cousin: "My daughter can't decide on her college major." Me: "It's normal for young people to be unsure about their future paths." Cousin: "She's torn between Communications and Psychology. What a waste." Me: "What do you mean by 'a waste'?" Cousin: "Both are useless. What kind of career will she have?" Me: "In my experience, with proper planning, people can excel in various careers. Many end up in fields unrelated to their college majors."

At this juncture, I sensed my cousin wasn't interested in genuine dialogue; he simply wanted to vent about his daughter's choices. Knowing my background in psychology, I suspected he was trying to provoke me. So, I tactfully addressed his negativity and defended my boundaries.

Cousin: "Well, you would say that. She should consider nursing. Something worthwhile." Me: "You seem quite critical of psychology. While everyone is entitled to their opinion, hearing such remarks, especially from you, who knows it's my profession, doesn't sit well with me. Can we shift to a different topic? Otherwise, I might have to chat with my dessert instead!"

A touch of humor helped diffuse the tension.

Cousin: "Uh, sure. So, have you picked out that new car yet?"

Was the conversation slightly awkward? Yes. Did I need to carefully assert my boundary? Absolutely. But did it resolve positively? Without a doubt! Moreover, I'm confident my cousin will think twice before subjecting me to his unwarranted negativity in the future.

Demonstrate Positive Conduct

A strategic approach to combating negativity involves setting an example of positive behavior. As discussed earlier in this chapter, while you can't control someone else's actions, you have full control over your own reactions.

However, if you can elevate your own happiness and inspire others to adopt a more positive outlook, it's a mutually beneficial outcome!

By consistently modeling positive behavior, you can achieve precisely that. You don't need to be excessively bubbly, but by consistently practicing the following, those around you who tend towards negativity might start to follow suit:

- Maintain a realistic perspective on situations while highlighting the positive aspects.
- Clearly establish your boundaries regarding what behavior you find acceptable from others.
- Stand firm in defending your personal boundaries.
- Take ownership of your emotions and reactions.
- Offer apologies when you unintentionally offend someone and seek to rectify any harm caused.
- Surround yourself with positive individuals as companions, friends, and acquaintances.

But what about those deeply entrenched in their negativity, holding onto it like a safety raft?

Here's where the modeling approach offers an additional advantage. While cynical, passive-aggressive individuals might scoff at your positivity, the good news is that they'll likely start to steer clear of you!

Happiness and optimism tend to discomfort such individuals, effectively acting as repellents to their negative influence.

11

Chapter 9: Identifying & Handling Love Addiction

Desiring a romantic relationship is natural, but some individuals become excessively fixated on love and romance. Love addiction can have detrimental effects on one's life, hindering the formation of healthy relationships.

While the term "love addict" is often tossed around casually in the media and self-help communities, its true meaning warrants examination. Here are the primary symptoms:

- **Obsession with Romance:** Constantly daydreaming about future partners, gravitating towards romantic media, and keenly following the love lives of others.
- **Belief in Love as Salvation:** Viewing falling in love as the ultimate solution to life's challenges, seeking refuge in fantasies where a romantic partner rescues them from all problems.
- **Viewing Social Occasions as Dating Opportunities:** Approaching every social gathering as a chance to find a love interest, constantly seeking someone who makes them feel special.
- **Jumping Between Intense Relationships:** Engaging in short-lived, intense relationships that fizzle out quickly, striving to establish deep connections rapidly and feeling euphoric when feelings are reciprocated.
- **Preferring Potential over Reality:** Attempting to mold partners into an ideal image rather than accepting them as they are, seeking to shape them into what one perceives as an ideal partner.
- **Fear of Singleness:** Experiencing loneliness at the thought of being single, often transitioning from one relationship to another without a break.
- **Dependence on Partner for Self-Worth:** Seeking validation and self-worth through relationships, feeling incomplete or lost without a romantic partner.
- **Reputation as a Love Addict:** Being labeled as a love addict or serial dater by friends and acquaintances, with others joking or expressing concern about one's tumultuous love life.

While infatuation in the early stages of a relationship is common, problems arise when love becomes the sole focus of one's life, overshadowing other important experiences.

Placing your happiness solely on someone else's reciprocation of your love is a risky endeavor. If they don't feel the same way, it can lead to heartbreak. In an attempt to ease the pain, one might hastily enter another intense relationship, perpetuating a cycle of emotional turmoil.

Ironically, these behaviors repel potential partners who are genuinely worthwhile. Few individuals would willingly involve themselves with a love addict once they recognize the situation, as it brings unnecessary drama into their lives.

Genuine relationships are not built on such unstable foundations. It's crucial to address love addiction seriously if you desire a healthy and fulfilling partnership. It's worth noting that love addiction isn't limited to crushes on familiar individuals. Some become fixated on celebrities or even fictional characters, showcasing the diverse manifestations of this issue.

Furthermore, love addiction affects both men and women, although societal norms may make it easier for women to discuss their feelings openly. However, men also grapple with similar challenges, even if they are less vocal about them.

While there are various theories about the root causes of love addiction, it's important to highlight one common aspect: the need to prove oneself to someone who may not reciprocate their feelings. Love addicts often stem from backgrounds of insecurity and lack of affection, seeking validation through relationships with narcissistic or emotionally unavailable partners.

Ultimately, love addiction isn't about genuine affection but rather about filling an emotional void and seeking approval that was lacking in childhood.

Overcoming Love Addiction

To recover from love addiction, you must embark on a journey that involves two fundamental aspects. Firstly, it necessitates the construction of an identity independent of the pursuit and retention of a romantic partner. This entails introspection into your relationship history, cultivation of personal interests, fostering a supportive social network, and the pursuit of ambitions and aspirations unrelated to love and romance. Seeking guidance from therapists, participating in support groups, or delving into literature authored by experts on love addiction, such as Susan Peabody's "Addiction to Love," can be invaluable resources in this endeavor.

Secondly, you must alter your approach to interpersonal connections. Authentic relationships cannot thrive if you consistently cast individuals into the role of your next great love. Establishing genuine connections requires removing the rose-colored glasses and adopting a patient approach to relationship-building.

Communication Strategies for Love Addicts

Develop proficiency in discussing everyday topics: Our conversations often reflect our priorities. For individuals grappling with love addiction, discussions predominantly revolve around relationships, crushes, partners, or ex-partners. However, incessantly dwelling on these themes tends to strain relationships in two significant ways.

Primarily, it diverts attention away from family and friends as the object of obsession consumes one's focus. Additionally, repeatedly discussing the same topic, such as romantic entanglements or relationship dramas, tends to alienate others. It's imperative to diversify conversation topics by cultivating hobbies and interests or by directing the discussion towards the other person's interests.

Exercise restraint in divulging personal details: Healthy relationships thrive on gradual disclosure of information. Love addicts, however, often divulge intimate details within a short timeframe, hoping to forge an immediate sense of intimacy. However, oversharing can have the opposite effect, as it

CHAPTER 9: IDENTIFYING & HANDLING LOVE ADDICTION

overwhelms potential partners and detracts from the natural progression of relationship development.

Master the art of engaging in casual conversation, learn to pose appropriate questions that foster healthy connections, and navigate relationships at a moderate pace.

Engage with individuals who will never pique your romantic interest as part of your journey towards overcoming love addiction. Cultivating friendships devoid of romantic potential is crucial for fostering positive relationships.

New friendships can be found in various settings, including the workplace, through mutual acquaintances, in educational settings, and within special interest groups. Challenge yourself to establish at least two new friendships with individuals you do not find physically or romantically appealing. Ideally, these friends should serve as examples of stable and contented relationships for future reference.

It's natural to initially struggle to invest in platonic relationships, as it takes time to overcome the notion that only romantic validation holds significance. Be patient with yourself as you navigate this transition.

Reduce reliance on digital communication methods such as texts and emails, and prioritize face-to-face interactions. Written messages often lead to over-analysis, triggering unnecessary speculation and misinterpretation. Opting for in-person conversations fosters genuine connection and minimizes the tendency to overanalyze interactions, a common pitfall for love addicts.

Recognize the crucial moment when it becomes necessary to sever all ties: For individuals grappling with love addiction, it's essential to grasp the art of cutting off contact with someone who triggers obsessive thoughts and behaviors. While numerous resources discuss the "No Contact Rule," its essence boils down to recognizing when someone exists solely as a fantasy or distraction and halting all interactions with them.

Clearly communicate to the individual that the dynamic no longer serves your well-being, signaling the end of the "relationship" with no calls, emails, texts, dates, or hookups. If professional or parental obligations necessitate interaction, maintain brief and courteous exchanges to avoid perpetuating the damaging cycle of on-off relationships common among love addicts. Acknowledge that this process is far from simple; it often entails a grueling journey.

Establish a robust support network to navigate through challenging emotions. Share your struggles with trusted friends, seek guidance from a therapist, or participate in well-moderated online communities to find solace and understanding.

Confront the reality of someone else's intentions: If you tend to delude yourself into believing that someone reciprocates your feelings solely based on wishful thinking, redirect your focus to their actions rather than their words. While anyone can send flirtatious texts, genuine interest manifests in consistent efforts such as showing up for planned dates or dedicating time for meaningful conversations.

Acknowledge that most romantic relationships do not stand the test of time, and attempting to salvage a failing relationship at the expense of your mental well-being is futile. Reflect on the fact that few individuals end up marrying their first love, and it's typical to explore multiple relationships before finding a lasting connection. Embrace this reality to cultivate a sense of security in your romantic endeavors, understanding that failed relationships do not define your worthiness or adequacy as a partner.

What should you do if you discover that you are in a relationship with a love addict?

Consider the scenario where you discover that the person you're dating is a love addict. Frankly speaking, it's not advisable to continue the relationship upon learning about their love addiction. If they confess to struggling with love addiction, it's a significant warning sign. Unless they are actively seeking help, whether through therapy or support groups like Sex and Love Addicts Anonymous, their unresolved issues are likely to sabotage your relationship.

Your partner may struggle to perceive both you and the relationship realistically, constantly seeking romantic highs and becoming distressed when their expectations aren't met. As mentioned earlier, no emotionally stable individual would willingly engage in a relationship with a love addict. If you identify signs of love addiction in your partner, it's essential to reflect on your own role in the dynamic.

Love addicts are often drawn to emotionally unavailable partners who offer sporadic affection and struggle with commitment. Therefore, it's crucial to ensure you're in the right mindset before entering into a relationship. If you're uncertain about your desires or whether you even want a relationship, you're more likely to attract individuals desperate for approval from someone unsure about providing it.

Take a step back and assess if you're truly ready to be emotionally vulnerable and open up to another person. If not, it's best to refrain from dating at this time. However, amidst the challenges of dealing with love addiction, there's an opportunity for self-reflection and growth. By examining your beliefs about relationships and developing strong communication skills, you can transform your struggles into a catalyst for personal development, paving the way for healthy connections in all aspects of your life.

12

Part II: Enhancing the Communication Abilities Necessary for Successful Relationships

13

Chapter 10: Understanding Different Communication Styles

Ever encountered a situation where you're conversing with someone, but it feels like you're speaking different languages? It's a common experience, and there's a straightforward explanation. In this section, we'll delve into why individuals have varied communication styles and how to establish a connection with anyone, irrespective of their way of communicating.

In the 1970s, psychologist Taibi Kahler delved into the correlation between an individual's personality type and their communication style. Initially focused on understanding negative thought patterns contributing to mental health issues like depression, Kahler sought to predict responses to therapy based on personality traits and communication preferences. His theory aimed to facilitate better connections in psychotherapy by grasping how individuals behaved under stress and their preferred communication style.

What makes this theory valuable is its applicability beyond therapy settings. It's beneficial for anyone seeking insights into why misunderstandings occur. If you find it challenging to understand someone, it could be due to differences in communication styles.

While this book equips you with skills to communicate effectively with any personality type, Kahler's model offers a valuable tool for comprehension. Identifying someone's primary personality type and communication approach can lead to smoother relationships once you understand them better.

The six primary personality types.

Kahler identified that individuals generally fall into one of the following categories. While nobody is confined to these patterns permanently, everyone possesses traits of these six personalities, each characterized by unique motivations and communication styles. However, most individuals tend to align more closely with one of these "types":

Harmonizers

[30% of Americans fall into this category, with 75% of Harmonizers being women] Here are some traits that indicate a Harmonizer:

1. They exhibit gentleness, compassion, and enjoy nurturing others.
2. They are sensitive and prone to being easily hurt.

CHAPTER 10: UNDERSTANDING DIFFERENT COMMUNICATION STYLES

3. They foster connections by sharing personal stories.
4. They excel at validating others.
5. They dislike solitude, preferring to assist and support others.
6. They appreciate visual arts, good food, and uplifting music, being highly receptive to sensory stimuli.
7. When upset, they become less assertive, experience a dip in confidence, and become flustered.

How to communicate effectively with a Harmonizer:

1. Offer affirmations like "You're incredibly generous" and "You're an excellent listener" to uplift them.
2. Engage in story exchanges, as Harmonizers appreciate openness.
3. Clearly articulate how they can assist and express gratitude for their help.
4. Maintain a calm demeanor and avoid escalating tension, as Harmonizers prefer peaceful interactions.
5. Display your gentle side to foster a sense of security.
6. Recognize signs of uncertainty and offer praise to bolster their confidence.

Thinkers

[25% of Americans belong to this category, with 75% of Thinkers being male] If you encounter a Thinker, you'll observe that they:

1. Prefer clear understanding of situations and timelines.
2. Value logical reasoning above all else.
3. Focus on facts and data.
4. Advocate for fairness, ensuring everyone's voice is heard in conflicts.
5. Favor solitude or small gatherings over larger social settings.
6. Become critical of others during stressful times and may exhibit pedantic behavior regarding details like dates and schedules.

How to effectively communicate with a Thinker:

1. Be direct and provide factual information upfront.
2. Earn their respect by supporting your arguments with objective facts and figures.
3. Acknowledge and praise their diligence rather than focusing solely on their personality traits.
4. Opt for one-on-one communication whenever feasible.
5. When addressing concerns, present factual evidence and list your feelings concisely.
6. Leverage their strengths by seeking their assistance in planning or research tasks.
7. Be prepared for meticulous behavior and redirect discussions back to the main issue if necessary.

Persisters

[10% of Americans fall into this category, with 75% being male] Identifying traits of a Persister:

1. They possess keen observational skills.
2. They quickly discern essential facts in any situation.
3. They express their opinions firmly and uphold their values.
4. They are conscientious and dislike leaving tasks unfinished.
5. They tend to be introverted.
6. Under stress, they may become overly assertive, especially regarding their belief system.
7. They have high expectations of themselves and others.

Effective communication strategies with a Persister:

1. Demonstrate respect for their cherished beliefs, even if you disagree.
2. Acknowledge and commend their completed tasks.

CHAPTER 10: UNDERSTANDING DIFFERENT COMMUNICATION STYLES

3. Address problems in terms of beliefs and values, as they place great importance on personal convictions.
4. If debating with a Persister, express a genuine desire to understand their beliefs.
5. Establish and defend your boundaries, particularly when faced with dogmatic behavior.
6. Engage in private or small-group conversations, as they prefer intimate settings over large gatherings.

Imaginers

[10% of Americans belong to this category, with 60% being female] Indicators of an Imaginer:

1. They maintain composure while expressing their thoughts openly.
2. They exhibit creativity and propose multiple solutions to problems.
3. They are predominantly introverted and prefer solitude.
4. When encountering problems, they may experience analysis paralysis.
5. They struggle to seek help when needed.

Tips for effective communication with an Imaginer:

1. Respect their need for solitude and give them time to process situations independently.
2. Offer assistance multiple times, as they may hesitate to accept help initially.
3. Present situations concisely and explicitly request their assistance when seeking a solution.
4. Appreciate their problem-solving abilities and unique perspectives.

Rebels

[20% of Americans fall into this category, with 60% being female] Common traits of a Rebel:

1. They exhibit high energy levels and are enjoyable to be around.
2. They demonstrate creativity and enjoy spending time in groups.
3. They have a competitive nature and strive to excel.
4. They tend to judge others quickly and avoid admitting personal faults.
5. While generally upbeat, they can become negative when things don't go their way.

Effective communication strategies with a Rebel:

1. Match their energy level to establish rapport, as they respond well to enthusiasm.
2. Show appreciation for their sense of humor and approach problem-solving as a game whenever possible.
3. Acknowledge and praise their imaginative efforts.
4. Offer choices between multiple options, allowing them to express preferences.
5. Prepare for potential blame if delivering unfavorable news.
6. Maintain your boundaries against their negativity.

Promoters

[5% of Americans belong to this category, with 60% being male] Identifying features of a Promoter:

1. They prioritize knowing future events and actions.
2. They value action over contemplation and enjoy winning.
3. They excel at persuading others and thrive in group settings.
4. They may use charm to manipulate others and can become bored easily.

Effective communication strategies with a Promoter:

CHAPTER 10: UNDERSTANDING DIFFERENT COMMUNICATION STYLES

1. Keep discussions grounded in reality rather than focusing solely on dreams.
2. Allow them opportunities to showcase their knowledge and skills.
3. Appreciate their charm and flattery within reasonable limits.
4. Safeguard against manipulation by maintaining firm boundaries.
5. If detecting boredom, promptly obtain necessary information or commitments from them.

How can this model be beneficial to you?

As demonstrated, each personality type offers a unique perspective on the world. Upon reading the descriptions, you likely associated individuals you know with these categories. Now, consider the potential conflicts that arise when individuals with differing personalities must collaborate or coexist. It can lead to complications. However, armed with this knowledge, you can devise effective strategies.

The Persister and the Promoter Allow me to illustrate how this theory aids in understanding and interacting with others. Personally, I identify as a Persister – steadfast in my beliefs, observant, and committed to completing tasks. A while back, I went on a few dates with a Promoter. At the time, I was delving into personality theories, offering a firsthand glimpse into the practical application of this model.

My date possessed the lively, charming, and organized traits typical of a Promoter, which complemented my personality well. As outlined earlier, Promoters may resort to manipulation when their desires are thwarted. During our second date, she recounted a story about manipulating a colleague, leading to his dismissal. This raised a red flag for me. Ordinarily, I might have ended the relationship, but I was intrigued to observe the situation unfold.

One evening, she called me ostensibly to inquire about my day. However, the conversation took an unexpected turn: HER: I'm relieved your day went smoothly. Mine wasn't great. ME: Oh, what happened? HER: It's nothing, really. ME: Alright. [At this point, I sensed a shift in our interaction.] HER: Actually, let me tell you. [Deep breath, audible swallow.] You know my cat, Monty? I had to take him to the vet today. He's really sick and needs surgery, which I can't afford. ME: That's awful. Poor Monty. When is his surgery scheduled? HER: That's the issue. It costs six hundred dollars, and I don't have insurance. Could you lend me half? [I had known her for only three weeks and was not inclined to lend money. Firmly, I declined, insisting she seek alternative solutions.] HER: Typical. You're selfish. I've been kind to you, but you only care about yourself. I'm reconsidering whether I want to see you again. ME: That's regrettable. I believe our conversation ends here.

Fortunately, I anticipated such behavior, given her Promoter traits and prior admission of manipulating others. While I didn't foresee the specific request for money, her attempt at emotional manipulation didn't surprise me. Interestingly, she had never mentioned Monty before. It's uncertain if Monty even existed. I'm not implying that Promoters are inherently negative; rather, awareness of diverse personality types, coupled with personal observations, empowers you to navigate relationships, particularly with toxic individuals.

Applying the model to resolve conflicts.

This method is most effective when both parties are familiar with the model and have previously discussed it. Consider a scenario where you identify as an Imaginer, while your partner is a Rebel. As an Imaginer, you prefer solitude to contemplate a situation rather than immediately seeking resolution with your partner. On the other hand, your Rebel partner prefers a direct approach, aiming to brainstorm creative solutions together.

However, by acknowledging the contrast in your communication styles, you can find a middle ground. For instance, you might agree to take some time alone to gather your thoughts before convening to brainstorm potential solutions within a set time frame, such as 10 minutes. This approach

CHAPTER 10: UNDERSTANDING DIFFERENT COMMUNICATION STYLES

accommodates the Imaginer's need for solitude during moments of stress while fulfilling the Rebel's desire for collaborative and creative problem-solving.

Why not utilize this chapter as a springboard for a discussion with your partner about your respective communication styles? It could mark the beginning of a more constructive and harmonious phase in your relationship.

14

Chapter 11: How to Validate Another Person (And Yourself!)

Beyond security and trust, what individuals desire most in their relationships can be summarized in one word: Validation. As social beings, we crave acceptance for our true selves. This aspect holds particular significance in romantic relationships, given their intimate nature. When our partner fails to acknowledge our perspective or support us during challenging times, it can lead to feelings of hurt. Validation serves as a simple yet profound way to communicate unwavering support to your partner, once you grasp its underlying principles.

But what exactly is validation?

Have you ever left a conversation about a complex or sensitive topic feeling truly understood by the other person? It's a wonderful feeling when someone comprehends your viewpoint, even if they don't necessarily agree with it. Validation signifies that someone genuinely values who you are and what you strive for. Whether you're navigating a disagreement or discussing a tough situation, validation serves as a vital foundation, fostering rapport and mutual respect.

It's important to differentiate between empathy and validation. While empathy entails understanding another person's perspective by placing yourself in their shoes, validation goes a step further. To validate someone means not only grasping their viewpoint but also wholeheartedly accepting them as they are. Instead of simply reflecting their emotions, validation involves providing concrete reasons for understanding their position and acknowledging its validity. The most potent combination is empathy coupled with a generous dose of validation.

Still uncertain? Let's delve into an example that illustrates the distinction between empathy alone and empathy complemented by validation.

Empathy in practice PARTNER

You didn't call me when you said you would. Do you not care about my feelings? I'm feeling hurt right now. YOU: I understand. I realize that my actions have deeply upset you. I apologize.

Empathy combined with validation in practice PARTNER

You didn't call me when you said you would. Do you not care about my feelings? YOU: I understand your perspective, and I acknowledge that I've caused you distress. I apologize. I recall last month when you shared how neglected you felt in your previous relationship when your ex delayed returning your calls. Additionally, I recognize that my tardiness last week exacerbated your concerns. I comprehend why it seems like I'm indifferent, and I empathize with your emotions. Rest assured, I value your feelings, and I'm eager to make amends. The latter response demonstrates deeper consideration. It avoids defensiveness and conveys a sense of importance to the other person.

Evidence supporting the impact of validation Still skeptical? Research underscores the significant influence of validation. In a study conducted by two Korean psychologists, validation proved superior to empathetic responses in enhancing participants' self-esteem and reducing their aggression. The researchers enlisted 80 participants for a computer game experiment. Through covert computer programming, some participants were led to believe that other players were excluding them from the game. These participants were then divided into three groups. One group listened to a neutral recording containing factual information about the game.

The second group heard empathetic statements describing the emotions they might have felt due to the perceived exclusion. Lastly, the third group listened to a recording that not only outlined the possible feelings but also validated them. For instance, this group heard: "Given that you felt distressed in this situation, you likely desire harmonious relationships and consider a sense of belonging and closeness with others significant." While both the empathetic and validation scenarios improved the participants' feelings regarding exclusion, the validation approach proved more effective.

Validation Techniques

Offer Hypotheses When Emotions Are Unclear: Sometimes, individuals may struggle to articulate their feelings, particularly if they're experiencing conflicting emotions. Without a clear understanding of their emotions, complete validation becomes challenging. To address this, assess both their verbal expressions and nonverbal cues, then employ the following phrases to delicately propose potential emotions: "It seems like you might be feeling..." "Based on what I'm hearing, it appears that your predominant emotion right now is..." "Do you think you're experiencing...?" Even if your assumptions are incorrect, the individual can provide clarification. In fact, identifying what they aren't feeling can help narrow down their actual emotions. By maintaining patience and validating whatever emotions they express, this strategy fosters mutual comprehension.

Pose Clarifying Inquiries: Mere repetition of someone's statements alongside generic validation may signal a lack of genuine attentiveness. To counter this, ask one or two probing questions and attentively listen to their responses, even if you already possess the answers. This approach enhances the sincerity of your validating remarks. For instance, suppose your partner has been juggling multiple work projects and expressing frustration with their manager's incompetence.

PARTNER: Oh, it was a dreadful day at work! Our team leader dismisses all our suggestions, despite the project heading towards chaos. YOU: It sounds like you're feeling frustrated. Could you specify which project you're referring to? PARTNER: It's the upcoming marketing campaign. It's incredibly stressful, with a mountain of tasks to complete. YOU: I understand this is causing you significant distress. Clearly, you're feeling overwhelmed. Given the recent challenges you've faced at work, it's entirely understandable.

In conversations like these, it's crucial to pinpoint exactly what is troubling your partner. If you're unsure of the root cause of their distress, your attempts at validation and empathy may come across as condescending or detached.

Reflect on past events when appropriate. Events don't occur in isolation, so if you're puzzled by the intensity of your partner's reaction, consider past experiences that may have shaped their current perspective.

Sometimes, normalizing their emotions can be comforting. Many people appreciate knowing that their reactions are not unique and that others have similar responses to certain situations. For instance, if a friend expresses anxiety about starting a family, you might respond by acknowledging the common apprehension associated with such a significant life change.

However, there are instances where normalizing emotions is inappropriate. In particularly sensitive or traumatic situations, reassurances about the normalcy of their feelings may come off as patronizing. Likewise, it's not advisable to normalize emotions when someone's behavior is widely considered unacceptable or unethical. For example, if your partner has acted inappropriately at work, such as shouting at a customer, it's not appropriate to suggest that their behavior is typical or justified.

Ensure that your body language aligns with your words. Even if you're skilled at multitasking, it's important to give your full attention to your partner during validating conversations. Dividing your attention may convey insincerity or a lack of seriousness about the situation.

Avoid passing judgment on their choices. Validation doesn't require agreement; you can validate someone's feelings even if you hold a different perspective. However, critiquing their choices undermines the validation process. If you find yourself inclined to offer advice or judgment, take a brief break to shift from a judgmental mindset to a validating one. Wait until they've shared their perspective before offering any advice.

Inform them that while you were attentive to their words, you developed your own perspective. Inquire if they would be open to hearing your suggestions. It's crucial never to impose your viewpoint on others. Be cautious before simply saying "Me too!": While it can be reassuring to learn that someone else has faced a similar problem, it's essential to ensure that your experience genuinely aligns with theirs. Otherwise, you risk coming across as insensitive or uninformed.

Avoid suggesting quick fixes: It's natural to want to help someone you care about by offering solutions to their problems. However, jumping in with a solution without considering their feelings might make them feel invalidated. Instead of rushing to solve the issue, allow them to navigate their emotions first. Most people are capable of determining their own course of action.

Remember, the goal of validation is not to act as a savior but to empathize as a fellow human who understands their situation. Be mindful of "validation fishing": While everyone craves validation, some individuals are more subtle in seeking it. If your partner is direct in asking for your time and attention, that's wonderful. However, not everyone feels comfortable expressing their needs verbally.

This means you'll need to be observant for signs that they are seeking validation. These signs will vary from person to person, but they may include:

- Sighing or tutting when they're not in your line of sight – they likely want you to inquire about their well-being.
- Non-verbal glances or looks – they may be seeking feedback on an important matter.
- Joining you without any particular activity – they might be seeking a conversation to express their emotions.

How to Seek Validation from Your Partner.

When you find yourself in need of validation from your partner, the solution is simple: ask for it. However, it's not always as easy as it sounds.

Many of us have grown up believing that directly seeking validation is inappropriate and selfish. But let me assure you, it's not, as long as you're not constantly seeking reassurance from your partner. It's perfectly normal and healthy to occasionally ask them to validate your feelings and thoughts.

If this idea feels unfamiliar to you, don't fret. Here are a few phrases you can use:

"I'm feeling X about Y. Do you think my reaction is justified?"

"When X said Y to me, it really hurt. Would you have been hurt too?"

"I can't believe X did Y! It's quite shocking. Is it reasonable for me to feel upset about this?"

"I'm really proud of accomplishing X. I didn't think I could do it. Are you proud of me too?"

However, remember that asking a question when you're not prepared to hear the answer can be harmful. Only ask if you believe there's a reasonable chance that your partner can provide the validation you seek. If not, consider talking to someone else.

Self-Validation: Empowering Your Inner Dialogue

Consider this: What if you could provide yourself with the validation you seek whenever you needed encouragement? Throughout my life, I've learned to value the importance of maintaining positive inner dialogue. That inner voice, constantly commenting on our actions and emotions, can significantly impact our success in various aspects of life.

Failing to validate your own feelings leaves you susceptible to depression. While denying emotions may offer temporary relief in challenging situations, unresolved feelings can resurface later, causing greater distress.

For instance, imagine asking someone out on a date and receiving a rejection. Despite brushing it off and attempting to distract yourself, deep down, the rejection hurts. In such moments, it's vital to take time to acknowledge your feelings.

CHAPTER 11: HOW TO VALIDATE ANOTHER PERSON (AND YOURSELF!)

Self-validation and internal dialogue serve as powerful tools in navigating emotions and overcoming painful experiences. Conversely, self-invalidation fosters prolonged unhappiness.

Consider the following contrasting examples of internal dialogue:

Validating dialogue: "This rejection hurts. It's natural to feel this way since I genuinely liked them. Asking them out took courage, and it's reassuring to know my capabilities. There are other people out there whom I desire to be with."

"I feel like crying. Given my past relationships, it's understandable to doubt finding a partner. However, I can find contentment while single with some time for myself."

In contrast, self-invalidating dialogue includes phrases like: "Stop complaining. Others have it worse." "You're an adult; quit being pathetic." "Did you honestly think you had a chance? Face reality!" "I shouldn't be upset; there are plenty of other options."

Clearly, self-validating dialogue offers more constructive support, setting the stage for positive actions and fostering optimism. I encourage you to try monitoring your inner dialogue for just 24 hours, and you'll likely notice a significant improvement in how you feel about yourself and life. Mastering self-validation is a powerful tool for personal growth and well-being.

15

Chapter 12: How to Say "No" To Anyone

In a healthy relationship, both partners naturally aim to please each other. If you find yourself uninterested in your partner's happiness, it's worth reconsidering your decision to be with them. However, it's essential to recognize when this desire to please goes too far.

CHAPTER 12: HOW TO SAY "NO" TO ANYONE

If you struggle to assert boundaries and say "no," you may find yourself agreeing to things you're not comfortable with, leading to feelings of resentment. In the long term, if you're unable to communicate openly about how your partner's requests affect you, you may resort to passive-aggressive behavior as a way to express your hurt.

At the beginning of a relationship, it's common to go above and beyond for your partner. I vividly remember offering to shovel snow from my girlfriend's driveway every morning during a cold spell when we first met. Looking back, it seems a bit excessive, driven by the rush of hormones.

However, as the relationship matures, priorities shift. By our second anniversary, I might have declined such a request without feeling like a jerk. It wasn't that I had become selfish; rather, our relationship had evolved.

As we grow more acquainted with our partners and settle into the relationship, we become more grounded and realistic. We start evaluating whether the relationship is balanced by asking ourselves:

- Does my partner reciprocate the efforts I put into the relationship?
- Is there a healthy balance between giving and taking?
- Am I content with the current state of affairs?
- If not, what changes can I make?
- Do I feel empowered to influence the course of our relationship?

These questions hold significant weight and shouldn't be brushed aside casually. Consider this analogy: If you're unable to decline a request, your ability to genuinely say "yes" is compromised. A relationship built on unexpressed desires fosters inauthentic communication.

Thus, mastering the art of refusal is crucial. This skill extends beyond romantic relationships and proves invaluable in friendships and professional settings. My recommendation is to tailor your approach based on the nature of the request. Simplifying matters, I categorize requests into "reasonable" and "unreasonable."

Addressing reasonable requests involves considering requests that most people would find acceptable and appropriate. For instance, if your partner asks you to pick them up from the airport at 5 pm next Friday, given your flexible work hours, it's not an extraordinary request. While you may still need to decline, it's understandable for them to ask. Typically, we're willing to accommodate reasonable requests from loved ones, knowing they'd likely do the same for us.

Let's suppose you'd normally be happy to adjust your Friday schedule but have an exceptionally busy week, including a crucial client meeting at 4:30 pm. In this scenario, declining your partner's request becomes necessary. How can you navigate this situation to ensure both parties feel respected?

Begin with a positive note: Initiating the conversation with understanding and appreciation builds trust and maintains goodwill. For instance, saying, "I'd love to help you out, and it's always a pleasure to assist you..." sets a positive tone.

Offer a brief explanation for the "No" if possible: While "No" suffices as a complete sentence, providing a reason, especially for reasonable requests made in good faith, is considerate. Opt for concise, non-negotiable reasons like, "I have an unchangeable meeting," to justify your refusal effectively.

Provide an alternative solution or gesture of kindness to ease disappointment: While your partner may be disappointed if you can't assist them, offering an alternative form of support or a thoughtful gesture can help alleviate their disappointment.

By employing this strategy, you convey your care and concern for their well-being, even if you're unable to fulfill their original request. For instance, in

CHAPTER 12: HOW TO SAY "NO" TO ANYONE

the scenario mentioned earlier, you could suggest ordering a taxi for them or preparing their favorite meal to greet them at home.

Consider another situation, this time within a friendship dynamic. Suppose your best friend asks for your help in crafting wedding invitations for her upcoming ceremony, but you've already committed to visiting your parents. In response, you could say:

"I'd love to assist, but I've had plans to visit my family for weeks. However, I know Shelly enjoys crafting, and she might be available to help you this weekend. Have you considered asking her?"

"I'd be happy to help, but I've already arranged to visit my family. Although I can't be there in person, I'm willing to provide feedback if you send over some photos."

Both approaches allow you to uphold your own commitments while still offering support to your friend. It's important to note that this is a gentle refusal tactic, suitable for situations where you genuinely care about the other person and want to assist them.

However, if you prefer to give a direct "No," compromising may lead to feelings of resentment. In such cases, refer to the techniques outlined in the following section. Conclude with words of encouragement: Wrap up the conversation or note with warm sentiments that reflect your care and consideration. For example, if your partner requests you to pick up their son's medication on your way home from work but you're unable to, express your hopes for the son's speedy recovery and your anticipation for the weekend ahead.

Refuse to take responsibility for someone else's reaction: Occasionally, you may face negative reactions when declining a request, especially if you're known for being accommodating. Remember, as long as you've handled the situation reasonably, their response isn't a reflection of your character. Stand firm in defending your boundaries and asserting your right to be viewed as more than just a servant.

Declining unreasonable requests and dealing with difficult individuals

The aforementioned strategies are effective when dealing with reasonable requests within a positive relationship. However, as you're aware, there are individuals who take advantage of situations and disregard your needs for their own convenience.

For instance, imagine you've taken a week off from work, and it's only Tuesday of your vacation when your boss calls, acknowledging your time off but requesting you to come in the next day due to staffing issues. While you aspire for a promotion, you've also planned enjoyable activities for your remaining vacation days and don't want to be seen as overly accommodating.

In such situations, here are some guidelines to consider

Assert your boundaries by stating "personal rules": If you're asked to do something that contradicts your values or makes you uncomfortable, assert your personal standards firmly. Phrases like "I have a policy of not doing X" or "I never engage in Y" draw a clear line. If they press for explanations or criticize your stance, reiterate that these are your personal rules without exceptions. You can then subtly imply, "I trust you'll respect my boundaries," placing gentle pressure on them to act respectfully. Few people enjoy being perceived as disrespectful boundary-crossers.

Utilize the "broken record" technique: This method is effective for a reason. Repeat your response in the same tone until the other person understands your stance. If the situation allows for humor, jokingly suggest they get their hearing checked since you already declined the request.

Embrace silence: After providing your response, it's not your responsibility to steer the conversation. Don't feel compelled to fill silences with unnecessary explanations or apologies.

Beware of accepting "gifts": Be cautious if someone who doesn't typically show concern suddenly offers help or gifts. There's a possibility they're seeking something in return. Some may even wait before making their request known. Politely decline offers of assistance or gifts to avoid being caught off guard.

Employ a noncommittal phrase: When someone indirectly hints at needing help, respond with sympathetic phrases like "Oh dear" or "What a shame" without committing to assistance. This prompts them to clearly express their needs.

Offer advance praise: Conclude the conversation with encouraging words, expressing confidence in their ability to handle the situation independently. This demonstrates support while gracefully ending the discussion.

How to Decline a Date Invitation

Regardless of your communication skills or dating experience, navigating the realm of dating can often lead to awkward encounters. One of the most delicate situations arises when you need to reject someone's advances. It's a unique form of refusal because it feels deeply personal.

Receiving a rejection can sting, but delivering one isn't any more enjoyable. So, what should you say when someone asks you out, but you're simply not interested? Show appreciation: Asking someone out takes courage, so keep this in mind when declining. There's no justification for belittling someone. Always maintain their dignity and express gratitude for the invitation.

Consider your reputation: Avoid being labeled as callous or dismissive towards those who ask you out. A simple "No, but thank you" suffices. You're not obligated to provide a detailed explanation for your refusal in most cases.

If you genuinely like them as a person, opt for a softer approach: If the person asking you out is a friend or colleague you value but only in a platonic sense, honesty is key. Expressing admiration for their friendship while gently explaining your lack of romantic interest respects their feelings while maintaining transparency.

Avoid generalized statements about not seeking a relationship: Focus on rejecting the specific date or relationship proposal rather than implying a broader disinterest in relationships altogether. Doing so prevents misunderstandings and avoids leading the person on.

Never imply potential reconsideration: Offering vague responses like "I'll think about it" only prolongs the uncertainty for the other person. It's kinder to deliver a clear "No" and provide them with the space to process their feelings without false hope.

Recognize the importance of asserting boundaries: "No" is a powerful word that serves as a crucial tool for maintaining honesty with oneself and others. Learning how to utilize it effectively is essential for achieving genuine desires and fostering healthy relationships.

16

Chapter 13: How to Stop Having The Same Old Arguments

As relationships progress, it's natural to become more at ease with your partner, leading to increased security and deeper intimacy. However, you may also find yourselves repeatedly arguing about the same issues. This occurrence is common among couples and doesn't signify doom or incompatibility.

Understanding why these patterns develop and addressing them with effective communication strategies is essential for smoother relationship dynamics. Repetitive conflicts can gradually erode the joy and trust within a relationship, leading to doubts and exhaustion.

It's disheartening to learn that around 69% of issues in long-term relationships remain unresolved. However, there's hope. By recognizing your recurring patterns and addressing them proactively, you can resolve differences permanently.

Improving communication and prioritizing your partner's needs alongside your own are crucial steps in this process. Research indicates that the happiest couples maintain a positive-to-negative interaction ratio of at least 5:1. This means for every negative interaction, there should be five positive ones, fostering mutual fulfillment and longevity in the relationship.

Consider this: it takes numerous positive interactions to counteract the effects of a single negative argument. Therefore, investing in conflict resolution skills is vital for sustaining a healthy and fulfilling relationship.

Effective Strategies to Address and Prevent Recurring Arguments

Embrace Conflict: Contrary to common belief, disagreements within relationships are not inherently negative. It's the manner in which conflicts are handled that determines their impact. Avoidance or denial of issues only leads to simmering resentment and passive-aggressive behavior, ultimately driving a wedge between partners.

Identify Key Issues: Take the time, both individually and together, to pinpoint the top three recurring issues in your relationship. This exercise isn't about assigning blame or sparking new arguments but understanding the root causes behind ongoing conflicts. Recognizing shared concerns provides insight into areas that need attention and resolution.

CHAPTER 13: HOW TO STOP HAVING THE SAME OLD ARGUMENTS

Uncover Underlying Emotions: Look beyond the surface of arguments to understand the deeper emotions driving them. For instance, if a dispute arises over differing spending habits, delve into the underlying feelings at play. Perhaps one partner's desire to save stems from a need for security, while the other's spending habits are rooted in seeking relaxation and autonomy. By acknowledging these underlying emotions, couples can address core issues of security and mutual respect.

Exploring Root Issues:

To delve into underlying issues, ask probing "Why" and "How" questions until reaching the core problem. For instance: PARTNER 1: "I feel patronized right now." PARTNER 2: "Why?" PARTNER 1: "I dislike being told to budget more and spend less." PARTNER 2: "Why?" PARTNER 1: "Because it makes me feel belittled, like a child or fool. It suggests a lack of respect." While addressing practical financial matters is crucial, acknowledging Partner 1's sense of imbalance opens the door to discussing mutual respect needs.

Identify Triggers:

Recognize common triggers that escalate arguments, such as phrases like "You always..." or "I'm sick of this." These statements generalize issues or imply threats, diverting attention from the actual problem. Avoid using such phrases and refocus on the core issue to prevent conflicts from spiraling.

Implement Physical Changes:

Break habitual argument patterns by making physical adjustments during disagreements. Since body posture influences thought patterns, altering your physical position can disrupt negative associations. For example, if arguments often occur in a specific spot, consciously choose a different location to change the dynamics and facilitate more constructive communication.

Zero in on Specific Issues

Have you ever experienced an argument that escalated from a minor issue? Consider this scenario from my college dating days: ME: "You said you were free on Friday, but now you have to attend your best friend's party?" GIRLFRIEND: "Yes, that's correct." ME: "Were you aware of this earlier? It's Wednesday now! Didn't she invite you ages ago? I've made dinner reservations." GIRLFRIEND: "You're always so particular. Why can't we go out on Saturday instead?" ME: "That's not the point. It's not about the day; it's about you frequently canceling plans." GIRLFRIEND: "Well, guess what? You're always irritating me with your rigid schedules."

This disagreement initially centered on planning our next date but morphed into a broader argument about our perceived recurring behaviors. As expected, we ended up arguing about these broader issues rather than addressing the immediate problem, escalating the conflict. Had I kept the conversation focused on the date, we could have avoided the argument entirely. While I did have concerns about my girlfriend's habit of canceling plans, the timing wasn't appropriate to address them. Follow this fundamental guideline to prevent arguments from escalating: If the argument is about a specific issue, address that issue. If there's a broader underlying problem, agree to discuss it later.

Avoid Dwelling on Past Issues

Refrain from stockpiling past arguments and grievances to use against your partner during a dispute. It accomplishes nothing and only exacerbates anger and hurt feelings. Agree to Disagree: Accept that your partner may not always share your perspective. Embracing differences is a part of emotional maturity. Focus on working with reality rather than wishing for change and resenting your partner for being themselves.

Compromise for the Sake of the Relationship

CHAPTER 13: HOW TO STOP HAVING THE SAME OLD ARGUMENTS

After repeatedly having the same argument, prioritize reaching a resolution for the relationship's well-being. Winning every argument isn't essential; consider the bigger picture of your relationship rather than your ego. Stop Attempting to Change Your Partner's Mind: Recognize that you cannot force your partner to change their opinions. Instead, focus on choosing to tolerate their behavior and beliefs.

While it's undoubtedly painful, you might reach the realization that you and your partner are fundamentally incompatible. This leaves you with the difficult decision of whether to end the relationship, but at least you'll be basing your choices on reality.

Emphasize the Positive: Recall the 5:1 ratio? Approach your relationship issues from two perspectives. Actively address conflicts while also taking preventative measures to avoid issues from arising initially. Investing ample time together is crucial. While scheduled dates and conversations may not seem romantic, they are effective ways to accumulate positivity in your relationship's memory bank.

Verbal Repair: Implementing a simple strategy can significantly ease your partner's emotions. Even in the midst of constructive discussions, we don't always communicate fairly. However, opting for "verbal repair" during heated exchanges can prevent long-term resentment. Although it might challenge your ego, a few words can make a substantial difference. Here are some examples:

- "Sorry, let me try a different approach."
- "Sorry, I'll rephrase my statement."
- "I realize I overreacted. Can we start over?"
- "I see I've hurt your feelings. Can I try to explain differently?"
- "I recognize my mistake. Can I clarify my point?" Remember, your tone is as crucial, if not more so, than your words. Avoid sarcasm or a patronizing tone. If you find it difficult to speak respectfully, it's better to take a break

from the conversation.

What if these methods prove ineffective?

The guidance provided in this chapter is rooted in robust psychological research. However, I understand that resolving issues alone may not always be feasible. Consider seeking professional assistance if:

- Your partner is unwilling to collaborate on resolving your issues.
- Your disagreements escalate into violence or abuse.
- Everyday communication has deteriorated, making it challenging to discuss anything.

When a relationship begins to deteriorate, swift action is essential to prevent permanent damage to its foundation. When recurring arguments leave both parties feeling unheard, either or both partners may become indifferent. While one person may attempt to sustain the relationship, if one partner has silently given up, continuing may be futile. Upon suspecting that counseling is needed, schedule a session with a therapist. Explain to your partner why you believe seeking help for your relationship is necessary and inquire if they would be willing to join you. Unfortunately, they may decline therapy or deny any issues.

Nonetheless, attend the session. Therapists specialize in assisting individuals facing relationship challenges and can offer guidance on the next steps, whether individually or as a couple. While I advocate for salvaging relationships, it's unrealistic to expect every partnership to succeed. There is no shame in ending a relationship with a partner who fails to meet your needs, is abusive, or has given up. Your partner should uplift you, not bring you down! Ultimately, prioritize your needs. Respect yourself and avoid remaining in a relationship that negatively impacts your mental well-being!

17

Chapter 14: Topics Couples Fight About Most Often

At this stage, you likely understand how skills like validation, assertiveness, managing repetitive arguments, and respecting differences in communication styles can effectively address various relationship challenges.

In this chapter, my goal is to offer practical advice for resolving common relationship issues. While compromise may be necessary at times, it's a preferable outcome compared to ongoing conflict and resentment.

So, what are the most common topics that couples tend to argue about? Renowned relationship expert John Gottman, along with his wife Julie, who operate the Gottman Institute in Seattle, have extensively researched romantic relationships for over four decades, providing valuable insights.

According to Gottman, the top five issues that couples frequently argue about are:

- Physical intimacy
- Extended family
- Free time
- Money
- Housework

This list encompasses nearly all aspects of daily life. Even though "Career" and "Work" aren't explicitly mentioned, disputes regarding money and free time often indirectly involve these areas.

Within these categories, numerous subtopics can serve as the basis for disagreements. For instance, under "Extended Family," issues with parents, in-laws, siblings, and other relatives can arise, contributing to common "family issues."

Regarding physical intimacy, there's a common stereotype that men typically have higher libidos, but this isn't always the case. Therapists frequently encounter situations where wives express concerns about their husbands' decreased interest in them.

In relationships with mismatched libidos, the partner with a higher sex drive may worry that their attractiveness is questioned, while the less interested partner may feel pressured into intimacy.

How can you narrow the disparity in libido between partners?

Assess libido levels:

Therapist Seth Meyers suggests a numerical ranking system from 1 to 10, with 1 representing a low libido and 10 indicating a high libido. By understanding each other's ranking, couples can depersonalize differences in libido, fostering a more objective approach. For instance, if one partner rates themselves as a 7 and the other as a 4, it becomes clear that expectations should align with each person's libido level. Recognizing this can initiate a constructive compromise.

Establish intimacy schedules:

Despite external stressors affecting both partners' libidos, scheduling intimacy, although it may seem unromantic, can prioritize it in their relationship once again.

Explore desires openly:

While discussing sexual desires can be challenging, it's crucial for a healthy long-term sex life. If face-to-face conversations are daunting, alternative methods like writing letters or emails can facilitate communication. When both partners feel listened to and acknowledged regarding their sexual preferences, they are more inclined to engage physically. This dialogue can lead to the creation of a shared list or "menu" of activities both partners are comfortable with.

Extended family dynamics.

While jokes about in-laws often exaggerate, they typically stem from some truth. Considering many individuals already grapple with familial issues, integrating into another family can be challenging. Here are strategies to navigate familial tensions effectively:

1. Proactive disclosure: Share any familial challenges with your partner as you both learn about each other's family backgrounds. Knowledge fosters understanding and equips you both to handle potential conflicts better.
2. Unified approach: When familial issues arise, discuss them with your partner and mutually decide on a course of action. Consistency in your responses garners respect, so avoid contradicting each other in front of family members. Instead of presenting ultimatums, strive for compromise and balance between family ties and your relationship.
3. Historical perspective: Understand that you're not merely encountering individuals but engaging with a family's intricate history and dynamics. If family dynamics seem unusual or toxic, recognize that past events may have influenced them. Refrain from assuming responsibility for family issues and maintain neutrality, especially when hearing conflicting accounts.
4. Reserve judgment: Take the time to familiarize yourself with your partner's relatives before forming conclusions. Initial impressions can be misleading, so refrain from relying solely on hearsay and instead engage with family members directly to form your opinion.
5. Assess relationship viability: If maintaining contact with certain relatives proves detrimental to your well-being and there are no legal or moral obligations dictating otherwise, it's acceptable to sever ties. Respect is paramount, and if boundaries are consistently disregarded, it may be necessary to distance yourself from toxic familial relationships.

Leisure time management.

Balancing work, childcare, and personal time can be challenging for many couples, often leaving one partner feeling deprived of individual space. How can you negotiate the allocation of leisure time between shared and solo activities? Here are some strategies:

Schedule dedicated "couple time"

Agree on a reasonable amount of shared time, mark it on your calendar, and commit to it. This approach provides both partners with something to anticipate and helps prevent disputes about neglecting one another. Joint activities, ideally, should be enjoyable and contribute to building intimacy and positive memories.

For instance, while productive tasks like painting the living room may be necessary, they may not foster the same level of connection as more leisurely activities.

Respect your partner's need for solitude

Acknowledge that everyone requires personal space for introspection and pursuing individual interests. Avoid questioning your partner excessively about their solo activities, as this can infringe upon their autonomy.

Cultivate personal interests and discuss them openly

Spending all leisure time together can lead to monotony and staleness in the relationship. Encourage each other to develop separate hobbies to allow for personal growth and diversify conversation topics. This not only provides breathing room but also enriches your interactions with new experiences and perspectives.

Financial Management.

Managing finances is a common source of tension for many couples, and for good reason—how you handle money can significantly impact your lifestyle and future financial security. If you struggle to discuss finances with your partner, it can lead to serious problems down the road.

- Establish transparency early on: Financial compatibility is crucial for a successful long-term relationship. Avoid sugarcoating financial realities and be upfront about your lifestyle expectations from the outset. Before moving in together, have an open discussion about your financial situations and agree on financial responsibilities.
- Discuss hypothetical scenarios: Address potential challenges, such as job loss or other financial setbacks, beforehand to minimize stress and uncertainty in the future.
- Ensure both partners have autonomy: Dictating how every penny is spent can breed resentment. Establish a budget that allows each person to maintain some level of financial independence. Even a modest monthly allowance can provide autonomy and flexibility without the need for constant justifications.

Household Responsibilities

Household chores are rarely anyone's favorite activity, and when there's a perceived imbalance in the division of labor, tensions can rise. Here's how to ensure a fair distribution:

- Define your priorities: Determine whether you both have similar cleanliness standards or if one of you has higher expectations. Find a middle ground on what constitutes an acceptable level of cleanliness.
- Create a chore list and schedule: Identify tasks that need to be done regularly and divide them based on each person's abilities and preferences. Flexibility and compromise may be necessary.
- Designate a set "housework hour": Agree on a specific time each day to tackle chores together if creating a schedule seems daunting.
- Address non-cooperation at week's end: Review the chore schedule weekly and discuss any issues if one partner isn't fulfilling their responsi-

bilities. Utilize assertive communication and boundaries if needed.

Remember, effective communication is key to resolving these issues. Rather than trying to tackle everything at once, focus on addressing one or two concerns each week in a constructive manner with your partner.

18

Chapter 15: How to Use Communication To Rebuild Trust & Prevent Jealousy

As commonly acknowledged, individuals frequently betray each other's trust. Deception and dishonesty prove detrimental to any partnership as they gradually diminish the sense of security shared between two individuals. Adding to the complexity, jealousy frequently infiltrates relationships, exacerbating when one partner is discovered betraying the other. In this chapter, I will impart communication techniques aimed at enabling your relationship to endure instances of betrayal and irrational jealousy.

Rebuilding trust post-infidelity.

We're all acquainted with individuals who have either cheated or been cheated on. However, did you realize that, according to Statistic Brain, 14% of married women have engaged in infidelity with their spouses, while 22% of men have done the same to their wives? On a positive note, this suggests that the majority of individuals remain faithful. However, it's evident that infidelity is not an uncommon issue. Some individuals stray because they feel entitled and seek excitement. Consider the person who encounters an attractive new colleague at work and chooses to embark on an affair in pursuit of adding excitement to their life. Another scenario involves someone who feels flattered by romantic attention from a younger individual and consequently becomes entangled in an inappropriate situation due to excitement and curiosity.

Occasionally, someone may believe they are developing feelings for a third party, although this isn't a prevalent factor in affairs. More often than not, affairs occur because individuals lack the motivation or skills to address underlying issues within their relationship. Specifically, if you sense emotional or sexual deficiencies in your relationship and lack the ability to discuss these issues with your partner, you might be inclined to seek fulfillment elsewhere. On a positive note, proficient communication within a relationship reduces the likelihood of infidelity. But what steps should you take if infidelity has already occurred?

Communication strategies for repairing relationships

Establish clear agreements:

Defining boundaries is essential in addressing infidelity within a relationship. While physical betrayal is straightforward to identify, emotional infidelity or inappropriate interactions might blur the lines. To navigate this ambiguity, create explicit agreements together to rebuild trust and prevent future breaches.

These agreements should be detailed and documented to ensure clarity on acceptable behavior. Regular communication schedules further promote transparency, fostering a sense of security for the betrayed partner. Even during seemingly smooth periods, scheduling regular catch-up sessions encourages intimacy and reinforces trust.

Prioritize stability and reliability:

Trust and security form the foundation of strong relationships. After betraying a partner, strive to exhibit composure, dependability, and consistency. Consistently honoring commitments, no matter how trivial, and openly sharing your schedule demonstrate your dedication to rebuilding trust. Similarly, if you've been betrayed, expect your partner to demonstrate these qualities as part of their efforts to reconcile.

Select confidantes carefully:

Dealing with infidelity is challenging, and seeking advice from others can add confusion. External opinions may sway judgment, complicating the resolution process. It's advisable to confide in trusted individuals who can offer support without imposing their views on the situation.

Reject drip-feeding:

Drip-feeding information, releasing details gradually, is detrimental to rebuilding trust as it prolongs the pain of betrayal. Embrace transparency by honestly addressing your partner's inquiries upfront. Conversely, if you've been betrayed, recognize drip-feeding as a manipulative tactic and demand full transparency.

Be open to revisiting discussions:

Rebuilding trust is a gradual process, and it's normal for the betrayed party to require multiple conversations to comprehend the situation fully. Patience and consistency in providing explanations are crucial in rebuilding trust. Avoid dismissing your partner's need to revisit the issue, as it may hinder progress.

Refrain from justifying betrayal:

Attempting to rationalize betrayal insults the betrayed partner and undermines accountability. While explaining motives is important, it should not absolve responsibility. If you've been betrayed, assert your right to end discussions if your partner attempts to justify their actions.

Allow time for healing:

Rebuilding trust is a prolonged endeavor requiring commitment and patience from both parties. Whether you're the betrayer or the betrayed, honesty about your emotions is vital throughout the process. Trust cannot be restored overnight, emphasizing the need for perseverance and understanding.

If you've experienced betrayal, there's no obligation to immediately forgive your partner. Pretending to have "moved on" while still enduring pain won't benefit your relationship. Similarly, if you've caused hurt, understand that your partner will require ongoing reassurance of your faithfulness and regret for an extended period. A mere apology won't suffice. If you find this responsibility overwhelming, ending the relationship might be the best course of action. Statistics indicate that only 31% of marriages survive infidelity, but effective communication serves as a pathway to restoring functionality. While professional therapy may be necessary for complete recovery from an affair, the strategies outlined in this chapter offer a solid starting point.

Addressing Irrational Jealousy

It's essential to differentiate between rational suspicions of infidelity based on evidence and irrational jealousy devoid of factual basis. Overcoming irrational jealousy requires specific strategies:

- Avoid excessive reassurance or explanations: Continuously reassuring a jealous partner or meticulously detailing your activities won't alleviate their doubts. Irrationally jealous individuals aren't swayed by logic. Similarly, if you're the jealous one, recognize that trust is a choice and cannot be proven.
- Explore underlying causes through open dialogue: Previous negative experiences, such as abusive relationships or childhood trauma, can fuel insecurity and mistrust. Discussing these issues can foster mutual understanding and empathy.
- Seek an objective viewpoint: Consulting a trusted friend for an outsider's perspective can offer clarity when assessing the reasonableness of jealousy, providing valuable perspective.
- Prevent fixation from becoming a habit: Excessive jealousy often stems from having too much idle time. Encourage healthy distractions and activities to redirect mental energy. Support your partner in finding constructive outlets without belittling their concerns.

While jealousy can be managed with effective strategies, excessive jealousy may necessitate professional intervention. Encourage your partner to seek therapy if their jealousy becomes overwhelming. Reluctance to seek help may indicate deeper issues that warrant attention for the well-being of the relationship.

19

Chapter 16: Communication Tools That Will Rekindle the Flame In Romantic Relationships

Love naturally evolves from passionate intensity to a more stable connection over time, but that doesn't mean you have to settle for monotony! This chapter offers quick tips to reignite the bond with your partner. The fundamental message is that meaningful communication can intensify emotions, revitalizing the relationship. Here are some ways to inject excitement into a seemingly stagnant relationship:

- Offer genuine compliments: Express admiration for your partner's attractiveness or achievements. A simple compliment can convey appreciation and respect, nurturing positivity in the relationship.
- Monitor negative comments: Increase the frequency of positive remarks while being mindful of critical or unhelpful remarks. Address issues with your partner in a constructive and affectionate manner, avoiding sarcasm or passive-aggressive behavior.
- Make "love vows": Rebalance the relationship by each committing to three loving gestures for the upcoming week or month. These pledges could involve tasks like giving a massage or preparing a favorite meal, fostering reciprocity and care.
- Schedule discussions on practical matters: Allocate specific time each week to address mundane issues like household chores or finances. This designated time ensures that such concerns don't overshadow the relationship's enjoyment.
- Write sincere appreciation letters: Express admiration for your partner's qualities and actions through heartfelt letters. Such gestures deepen intimacy and reaffirm love, strengthening the emotional bond.
- Exchange gratitude lists: Cultivate appreciation by compiling lists of things you're grateful for in each other. Sharing these lists regularly fosters gratitude and acknowledges the often-overlooked aspects of the relationship.
- Diversify communication channels: Experiment with different modes of communication, such as email or video calls, to keep interactions fresh and engaging.
- Implement tech-free hours: Dedicate time each day to disconnect from digital devices, promoting focused and attentive communication between partners.
- Maintain exemplary behavior: Continue displaying courteous manners

CHAPTER 16: COMMUNICATION TOOLS THAT WILL REKINDLE THE FLAME...

and considerate gestures to uphold mutual respect and admiration, reinforcing the initial impression made during the early stages of the relationship.

Why not revisit the excitement of the early days? Your partner will appreciate the effort you're making! We all have moments of taking our loved ones for granted, but it's simple to uplift your partner's spirits. If they inquire about your sudden kindness, be honest with them! Apologize for any lapse in effort compared to the earlier stages of your relationship and express your desire for them to feel cherished. There's no need for justification when it comes to demonstrating your love and appreciation for your partner.

20

Chapter 17: Effective Communication for Parents & Caregivers

In this section, I aim to offer additional guidance and insights for parents and anyone involved in the upbringing of children and adolescents. Having cared for my two young nephews extensively, I can attest that these suggestions greatly facilitate childcare!

CHAPTER 17: EFFECTIVE COMMUNICATION FOR PARENTS & CAREGIVERS

We've all encountered situations where we struggle to persuade a child to do something - whether it's finishing their meal, putting on their shoes, or going to bed - and they simply refuse to cooperate. Or perhaps you're trying to communicate with a teenager who seems unresponsive. Regardless of age, communicating effectively with kids can be challenging.

Here are some key principles to keep in mind:

1. Avoid yelling: While yelling might provide temporary relief, it's ultimately counterproductive. It teaches children that it's acceptable to respond aggressively when they're upset, which isn't conducive to healthy communication. Furthermore, yelling triggers defensive reactions in both parties, shutting down communication channels.
2. Offer choices: Children often feel frustrated when they constantly receive directives from adults. Part of their development involves establishing a sense of autonomy, which is hindered when they have no say in matters. Try to strike a balance by guiding their behavior while allowing them to make choices within reasonable boundaries.
3. Utilize transition times for conversation: Children and teens tend to be more relaxed during activities like car rides or mundane tasks, making these moments opportune for meaningful conversations. Pay attention to these opportunities and encourage them to share their thoughts and feelings.
4. Allow room for mistakes: While it's natural to want to impart wisdom, it's essential to let children learn from their own experiences. Unless they're in immediate danger, resist the urge to intervene unnecessarily. Instead, offer guidance when solicited, respecting their autonomy.
5. Model emotional expression: Demonstrate healthy ways to express emotions by openly discussing your own feelings with children. This teaches them that it's normal to talk about emotions and that challenges can be overcome through communication and problem-solving.
6. Respect their perspective: Recognize that children have their own insights and feelings. When they express concerns, listen attentively

without interrupting, allowing them to express themselves fully.
7. Avoid judgmental responses: Criticizing children for their mistakes creates barriers to open communication. While it's crucial to establish boundaries and consequences, refrain from moralizing their actions excessively.
8. Clarify communication needs: If a conversation seems aimless, inquire about the child's preferences for the interaction. Understanding their communication style and needs enhances effective dialogue.
9. Start with observations, not questions: Instead of bombarding children with questions, initiate conversations with observations or thoughts. This approach feels less intrusive and encourages them to open up voluntarily.
10. Validate emotions: Rather than dismissing children's statements as irrational, acknowledge their feelings and inquire further to understand the underlying issues.
11. Explain your decisions: When imposing rules or making decisions, provide explanations rather than relying on authority. This helps children understand your perspective and fosters mutual respect.

By adhering to these principles, adults can cultivate healthy communication with children and adolescents, fostering trust and understanding in their relationships.

Here's an illustration:
CHILD: Can I stay over at Stacey's place on Friday night?
PARENT: Let me take a moment to consider that, and I'll give you an answer shortly, alright? [10 minutes later]
PARENT: I understand how much you enjoy being at Stacey's and how fun sleepovers can be, but we have plans to visit your aunt early on Saturday, and staying over might leave you too tired for that. So, this time, the answer is "No."
CHILD: But I really want to go!
PARENT: I know it's disappointing. However, there's a valid reason behind

CHAPTER 17: EFFECTIVE COMMUNICATION FOR PARENTS & CAREGIVERS

this decision, and it stands.

The fundamental principle here is to treat your child with the same respect you'd expect in return. Simultaneously, it's your responsibility to set and uphold reasonable boundaries. Despite common belief, children thrive on structure and consistency. Effective parenting involves maintaining a steady approach to discipline while upholding appropriate standards of conduct. Yet, it's equally vital to reassure children that you're there to offer support and guidance whenever needed.

21

Chapter 18: Communication Strategies for Friendships

While romantic relationships typically stand out as the most emotionally intense connections beyond our immediate families, friendships hold a significant place as well. For some, the end of a long-term friendship can be even more distressing than the conclusion of a romantic partnership, particularly impacting women, according to research.

CHAPTER 18: COMMUNICATION STRATEGIES FOR FRIENDSHIPS

So, what's the remedy? Well, it's no surprise - communication! While some friendships may naturally drift apart, understanding how to address common friendship challenges can fortify your bond and maintain closeness.

Let's delve into three common issues that often strain friendships and explore strategies to prevent them from causing a rift.

Issue 1: One-Sided Friendships

Unequal friendships can be disheartening. When you feel like you're investing more effort into the relationship than you're receiving in return, it can erode your self-esteem and confidence.

If the friendship is relatively new, it might be best to let it go. However, severing ties becomes more complicated when you've shared a long history.

I've personally experienced this dilemma. After college, one of my closest friends, Tom, continued to hang out with me every few weeks for years. The problem was, I was always the one initiating contact, leading to feelings of resentment. Despite my attachment to him, I struggled to contemplate cutting him off from my life, especially since our time together was enjoyable when it did happen.

So, how do you navigate such friendships?

Express your feelings:

While it seems logical that close friends would notice when their dynamic becomes imbalanced, some may remain unaware. Moreover, once a pattern forms where one person consistently takes the lead, the other may simply accept it as the norm. When I finally mustered the courage to confide in Tom about my feelings, he was genuinely taken aback. He had assumed I enjoyed being the organizer! Following our conversation, he made a concerted effort to change, and our friendship improved significantly.

Address their distance with sensitivity:

If your friend has been distant and unresponsive, it's possible they're dealing with personal issues. Approach the situation cautiously to avoid making assumptions or provoking defensiveness. Instead, express your concern for their well-being and convey that you miss them. Propose meeting up, which will reveal whether their behavior stems from neglect or circumstantial challenges.

Harness the power of scheduling:

After spending time with a friend, suggest planning your next get-together before parting ways. Express your enjoyment of their company and find a mutually convenient date. This eliminates the uncertainty of who will initiate the next hangout. Simply confirm the arrangement the day before. If they consistently cancel plans, it may be time to reevaluate the friendship.

Issue 2: Envy.

We'd all hope that our friends would share in our joy when we achieve milestones like getting a promotion, buying a new home, getting married, or landing our dream job. Unfortunately, jealousy can rear its head even among friends. Here are some strategies to address it:

Provide the full picture: Jealousy often stems from a skewed perception that someone else's life is perfect and devoid of problems. Counter this by being transparent about the challenges you face. For instance, if your friend is envious of your upcoming wedding, casually mention the stresses of dealing with in-laws and wedding planning. Avoid fabricating or exaggerating issues; simply convey that life has its ups and downs despite positive changes.

CHAPTER 18: COMMUNICATION STRATEGIES FOR FRIENDSHIPS

Share your joy with them:

Include your friend in your celebrations. If you've bought a house, invite them over for a special housewarming dinner. If you've had a baby, consider asking them to be a godparent. Similarly, involve them in milestones like starting a new job by seeking their input on outfit choices for your first day. Express gratitude for their involvement, reinforcing their importance in your life. This inclusivity can help alleviate their insecurity.

Take the lead in nurturing the friendship:

Envious individuals may feel sidelined by someone else's success. Provide reassurance by taking on a more proactive role in the friendship for a period. Make an effort to inquire about their life, prioritize spending time together, and offer genuine compliments. Avoid monopolizing conversations with your good news; instead, suggest new activities to explore together. View this challenge as an opportunity to strengthen your bond.

Issue 3: Breach of Trust.

Many of us have encountered situations where a friend engages in gossip or reveals deeply personal secrets, leaving us feeling betrayed and distant. How should you handle it when a friend violates your trust?

Seek understanding:

Rather than brushing aside the issue, it's essential to uncover the reasons behind their actions. Sit down with your friend, express your concerns, and ask for their perspective. While they may deny any wrongdoing, it's crucial to gather all relevant information to make informed decisions about the future of the friendship. Avoid relying on secondhand information; instead, address the matter directly, focusing on actions and consequences rather than personalities.

Prepare for defensiveness:

Few people are comfortable being labeled as betrayers, so expect your friend to become defensive. They might even attempt to shift the blame by highlighting your own shortcomings. Stay composed and refrain from escalating the situation. Stick to the facts and remain focused on finding a resolution for the relationship.

Mend the aftermath:

If your friend has spread falsehoods or shared secrets, you may need to address the damage with other individuals involved. For instance, if you suspect your friend has misrepresented your feelings to a third party, it's necessary to clarify the situation. While ideally, the friend responsible would rectify their actions, this outcome is not always feasible. Prepare to assess the extent of the harm caused and take steps to mitigate it. Rebuilding trust and reputation requires consistent, ethical behavior over time. Lean on trustworthy individuals for moral support during this challenging period.

Contemplating Forgiveness Towards Your Friend

The decision to forgive a friend for their misconduct ultimately rests with you. Recognize that nobody is flawless. To assist you in determining whether to salvage the friendship, consider the following questions:

- Overall, has this friendship positively impacted your life?
- Are there numerous joyful memories shared with this individual?
- Do both of you provide mutual support regularly?
- Would you deeply miss this person if the friendship ended?
- Do you believe you can openly discuss problems with this friend?
- Do you perceive them as fundamentally good but prone to error?

The more affirmative responses you can provide, the stronger the case for

CHAPTER 18: COMMUNICATION STRATEGIES FOR FRIENDSHIPS

forgiveness. However, remember that there are no strict rules obligating you to maintain ties with those who have mistreated you. Assessing the advantages and disadvantages of continuing the friendship is a personal evaluation that only you can undertake.

22

Conclusion

Now equipped with all the essential knowledge for nurturing a successful relationship, you might find the abundance of tips and techniques a bit overwhelming at first. That's okay! Consider highlighting the sections most pertinent to your relationship, and revisit them later for deeper understanding.

Let's review what you've gained:

- Understanding the dynamics of a healthy relationship and recognizing

CONCLUSION

societal influences that shape our perceptions of love and romance.
- Accepting that disagreements with your partner are inevitable and learning strategies to address common relationship challenges.
- Cultivating the right mindset for dating, selecting a compatible partner, and steering clear of codependent relationships.
- Clarifying your relationship preferences, asserting yourself when necessary, and mastering the art of saying "No."
- Sustaining excitement and novelty in long-term relationships.
- Developing effective communication skills with friends, family, and children.

Impressive, isn't it?

If you're currently in a romantic relationship, implementing the advice from this guide will likely yield noticeable improvements in just a few days. And if you're single, rest assured that you possess the ultimate toolkit for embarking on your quest for romance.

The Key Message.

A successful relationship requires active participation from both individuals, ideally with a strong sense of self-worth. Recognize your own value and demand respect from yourself and others. Adhering to this principle can shield you from toxic relationships and pave the way for genuine, enduring love.

My aspiration is that every reader of this book will find solutions to their relationship challenges through the theories and practical strategies presented here.

However, I acknowledge that some issues may require professional intervention. Nevertheless, even if therapy becomes necessary, this book can still serve as a valuable resource to fortify your relationship and prevent future issues. I extend my best wishes to you – I have faith in your ability to cultivate the fulfilling relationship you deserve. Here's to finding your own version of happily ever after!

www.ingramcontent.com/pod-product-compliance
Lightning Source LLC
LaVergne TN
LVHW021048100526
838202LV00079B/4891